T3248

WORKING IN TELEVISION

Working in
TELEVISION

JAN LEEMING

Batsford Academic and Educational Limited *London*

First published 1980
ISBN 0 7134 2248 3

Filmset by Progress Filmsetting, London
Printed and bound in Great Britain by
Redwood Burn Limited
London, Trowbridge and Esher
for the publishers
Batsford Academic and Educational Limited
4 Fitzhardinge Street, London W1H 0AH

Contents

Introduction

Most people are interested to know what goes on behind the scenes of the television screen and, when it comes to thinking about a career, I am sure many of you want to know what opportunities there are for the young person and how to find out more about the different jobs concerned.

You will realise that the medium of television is an extremely complex one owing not only to the great variety of work to be done before and during a programme but also to the importance which must be placed on the many and varied personalities involved who, whether they be programme planners, researchers, commentators, cameramen, engineers or interviewers, need to be able to work together as a harmonious team.

The complexity, with a certain amount in interchange and overlap of work and, indeed, with the different terminology used by the BBC and the independent companies for similar work makes it extremely difficult to write about any specific job in a straightforward way. It would be necessary to add each time that the circumstances given apply to a particular person rather than to a particular job, and may well be different for someone else!

I feel therefore that one of the best ways in which to introduce you to working in television is for me to tell you how I managed to enter the medium and my own experience of working behind the scenes as well as in front of the camera.

I have also invited a representative cross section of colleagues who work in other areas to tell you about their own jobs and to give you a few words of advice.

I hope that between us we have managed to convey the atmosphere of the world of television and that if you are seriously interested in becoming one of the team you will now have some idea as to which particular area would interest you most, and will write to one of the television companies to find out details of openings for young people and of their training facilities.

Although you will see that it is not essential to have high academic qualifications in order to be accepted for training by television companies, I would advise you while still at school, to take as many O level examinations as you can manage, and some A levels if at all possible. These qualifications do show that you have certain capabilities and may well save time in further study later on. But most of all, if you have talent and/or flair for a particular job and are determined to make it you will be given every opportunity.

There is of course a vast number of secretaries and clerical workers who are invaluable to the team and new recruits are in constant demand. So if you really want to share the atmosphere of working in television but do not feel you can be a technician, a producer or perhaps an interviewer, there may well be an opening for you among the secretarial or clerical staff. You can read about secretarial duties in the title *Working as a Secretary* by Angela Wilson, also in this series of career books.

It is possible too that if you have talent and a certain amount of work such jobs may well lead on to work more directly involved with the transmission of a programme.

I must stress the importance of dedication to the job. The work is hard, the hours long—but the job satisfaction is great.

Acknowledgment
My sincere thanks are due to all those people who have helped in the preparation of this book and to those who have willingly filled in questionnaires about their own jobs, adding a word of personal advice as well as a touch of humour.

J L 1980

8

Personal experience

I cannot say 'I always wanted to work in television' because when I was a little girl very few people actually possessed television sets. My family was among the vast majority who did not but we occasionally caught a glimpse of a magic box belonging to someone else. Imagine that! Going to see a relative or friend who did have a television was quite a treat even though it was only black and white and the reception fell far below today's standards. That is an understatement—in fact most of the programmes were viewed through what looked like a continual snowstorm. But we accepted it, 'snow' and all.

I don't suppose it would have entered my head to consider a career in television because there were so few programmes in those days and women were mainly used as announcers; and after all, most girls became nurses or secretaries, or if they were terribly daring they went into the theatre. And that's just what I wanted to do—'wanted' being the operative word.

Heaven knows where my desire to be an actress originated: I was an end-of-the-war baby (1945, not 1918!) so theatrical treats were thin on the ground for many years. The actors were mostly doing their share of war work or had gone away with ENSA to entertain the troops, and it took time and money to re-establish the theatre at home. I might add that many of today's famous artists began their careers in far flung corners of the British Empire—we had one then! I've tried to trace someone within my family who may have had theatrical leanings and have only come up with an extremely distant cousin who lived in India in the days of the Raj and who played the piano. As for me, well, my thespian beginnings were very humble. I began, at the age of five, by boring relatives and friends alike with my one-person rendition of that well-known fairy tale, *Rumplestiltskin*. I played all the parts of course and must have looked mad as I chased across the living-room floor to play first the dwarf and then the princess.

Personal experience

So what has all this got to do with a career in television? I always had a flair for acting but decided that I didn't have the temperament (and maybe not the talent) to take the tremendous insecurity of a theatrical life. I was interested in people from all walks of life and I hated routine. All I had to my credit was a pretty good education and secretarial qualifications, so where next? I applied to the BBC and after completing a fairly rigorous test was taken on as a secretary in the Programme Correspondence Section...you see, people do exist to deal with the many brickbats and occasional bouquets handed out by the listening and viewing public. For every one person you see on your screen or hear on the radio, there are literally hundreds beavering away behind the scenes; secretaries, researchers, producers, editors, film editors, film cameramen, lighting cameramen, floor managers, make-up artists, wardrobe mistresses, accountants, and engineers, to name but a few. The point I am making is that there are very many different career avenues in television. If I tell you my story first, you will see that a career structure in television, particularly that of an interviewer, hardly ever runs in straight, and never runs in smooth, lines. You don't work at a job for a given period and then move on to another stage. It's not that simple. Television is a highly competitive, high-risk, hectic, nervewracking and very rewarding business. And by that last remark, I don't mean financially rewarding. Some people in television do earn a great deal of money but they are the exception, not the rule. Most people in the medium have interesting and creative jobs which are predominantly non-routine and there is a great deal to be said for job-satisfaction in this age of computerization.

School

Back to me. I began my scholastic careeer at an establishment known as The Assumption Convent in Charlton, South East London. At the time, I saw the place as a magnificent building dominated by an enormous statue of the Virgin Mary. A few years ago I went through Charlton on a sentimental journey, only to discover the Convent was now being used as offices and the building was really rather tiny after all. It was at Charlton that I launched myself on to the unsuspecting public for the first time. In front of a very select and captive audience of Mums and Dads I played King Canute, complete with cardboard crown and bath-towel royal robe over gymslip—very regal! We played to a packed house for all of one afternoon and the brilliant review we got in the school periodical spurred me on to greater things. My next starring role was as the wicked Queen in *Snow White and the Seven Dwarfs*. Please note my constant playing of regal roles! Mind you, my career practically came to an untimely end when the floodlight box toppled off the stage on to the floor below, being restrained only by the back of my foot which almost parted company from my leg. An unpleasant incident which was to be repeated with more gravity much later in my life. This meant that I was off school for a couple of months and unable to audition for the next epic at Assumption Productions. But by now there were more pressing things on my mind like passing my 11 plus. This I did quite well, I believe, gaining a scholarship to a Convent Grammar School in Abbey Wood, Kent. I forgot to mention that along the way my parents, unfortunately, had parted company. My father had done a stirling job looking after me for four years but as I was getting older the task was becoming more difficult, so he decided that I would go as a boarder to St Joseph's. There are some children who are mentally suited to boarding…I was not one of them. I loathe regimentation and even now hate being rudely awakened from my slumbers by any kind of alarm. All those years ago, our boarding mistress, a short and attractive nun, would stride through the dormitory like the prophet of doom swathed in black, ringing a great big hand bell and giving no quarter. Despite being a non-Catholic and also despite promises to my father to the contrary, I too was awakened at the ungodly hour of six, every second day, to attend mass. It wasn't the service I minded but the early rising. Just imagine our dormitory with cubicles down the middle for the 'big' girls and high hospital-type beds down the side for we little'uns. I used to long to be a 'big' girl, just to have the privacy of a cubicle, but it was not to be because after one short year, which seemed like an eternity, I became a day-girl. However, looking back on my boarding days, I suppose they weren't too bad and they do afford me the odd wry smile now and again. When I went to see the musical *Oliver* I was highly amused at the children holding out their dishes for more. Although as an adult I only ever eat a cooked breakfast if I'm travelling on a train…what is it about eating when one is bulleting through the countryside at eighty miles per hour—even if the food is indifferent, it's a magic sort of experience…well, at school when we'd been awoken at 6 o'clock and attended mass before breakfast, all of us were ravenous and I well remember how, on the days when we were lucky enough to have bacon, we used to jostle and push to get the congealing bacon fat handed out at the end of the meal…shades of bread and dripping! Sunday was an incredible day for boarders. We hardly got up off our knees! There was early morning mass followed by breakfast and no sooner was that over than we got ourselves ready for the walk to the local church. We must have looked rather smart in our special Sunday berets. They resembled the shape of a halo with gold braid on the rim as if to complete the effect of a holy circle. Off we'd troop in a crocodile two-by-two. Afterwards it was back to the Convent for lunch, play, homework, afternoon service, tea and, I'm fairly sure, another visit to the chapel for Benediction. I was greatly influenced by the theatricality of the religious services, received great kindness from and in turn loved most of the nuns and thought very strongly about converting. This desire diminished somewhat when I became a day-girl. Oh! incidentally, the only time I was ever late for school was when I was on the premises as a boarder.

My schooldays were fairly uneventful and I would be lying if I said they were the happiest days of my life because they weren't. However, I do think with great affection of the nuns who taught the 3 R's (reading, 'riting and 'rithmetic) and also the discipline they instilled into us. I know that 'discipline' is regarded as a dirty word in the vocabulary of so many people today but without it I don't think I would have worked as hard as I did at school. I wasn't academically brilliant by any means. I suppose you'd call me a plodder. I didn't excel at anything except English and Drama and was absolutely hopeless at games. But I did have a strong sense of competition in other directions and was always entering verse-speaking and drama festivals. I remember once being asked to stand in for someone who had gone sick a couple of days before a French verse-speaking contest. I had no idea what the words meant but I had learnt them by heart and had a convincing enough French accent to get through to the finals. I didn't win, but it was fun trying. Now I think about it, what cheek I had!

I was particularly fond of the nun who taught us English and we were fortunate to have her as our teacher throughout the five years at Grammar school. She had endless patience and was an excellent teacher. She used to organize many verse-speaking contests within our form during term time. I don't know whether it was a natural desire to show off, or to win her approval, but I remember for one of these form contests, I attempted to learn the whole of *The Ancient Mariner*. I came dreadfully unstuck and never attempted that kind of bravado again. Mother Mary David organised frequent trips up to The Old Vic at Waterloo so that we'd see Shakespeare in all his glory. I've still got all my little yellow programmes and memories of wonderful performances by young men and women, in many cases playing the traditional spear-carrying roles, who have now come to great prominence in the theatre and on film. To give you an example—in 1960 the Old Vic Company presented a production of *Romeo and Juliet* with Judi Dench and John Stride in the title roles but with people such as Tom Courtenay and Barbara Leigh-Hunt playing minute parts. I also remember seeing Paul Rodgers playing a magnificent Macbeth and on another never-to-be-forgotten occasion Richard Burton playing Othello to John Neville's Iago. Although I'm a great fan of Richard Burton, my heart-throb at that time was John Neville. I queued at the stage door for as long as Mother Mary David would let us, and nearly swooned on espying the wonderful Mr Neville in a navy and white spotted dressing gown. I didn't get his autograph on that occasion but wrote to him and was so thrilled to receive an autographed photograph—and it was *personally* signed. It still has pride of place in my autograph book. Although I never actually met and spoke to John Neville, I have had the great pleasure to meet and interview many of the folk I so idolized as a child—but more of that later.

Although I don't regard myself as any great scholar, authority deigned otherwise and I found myself in the 'Latin' stream at school. In those days, there were two streams doing precisely the same syllabus except for one notable exception. At the tender age of 11 the demarcation line was into the class which did cookery and everything else or the one which aspired to Latin and everything else. I really was dreadful at Latin and despite our wonderful Latin mistress, Miss Cronin, who selflessly gave up her lunch hours to take myself and a few other dummies for 'extra-Latin', I still failed my mock GCE miserably and didn't even make it through to the exam proper. Had I known then how very valuable Latin is in modern English word comprehension, I would have tried harder! At the time, however, I longed to be doing cookery with Mother Mary Patrick who made the most wonderful fudge I've ever tasted in my life and whose domain was an outbuilding away from the main body of the school—a place called Ker-Anna surrounded by rhododendron bushes and lovingly tended by Joe the gardener.

I became a day-girl after my first year at St Joseph's for two reasons. I really wasn't cut out for the regimentation of boarding-school life and was miserably home-sick even for the higgledy-piggledy home life which was the only kind my father could provide with my being parcelled off to courtesy aunts and uncles a great deal of the time. My father was in the army and in those days most army men had to do a stint abroad. He was posted to Singapore and asked my mother to come back and look after me while he was away, which she duly did.

I have already said that my school days were relatively uneventful. I had to work hard and was a very conscientious student. At the time, I often used to regret that I wasn't having as much fun as some of the girls but studying didn't come easily and when you think about it, those few school years are the formative ones for the rest of your life and there's plenty of time to have fun later.

In 1957 my father returned from Singapore and I sat for seven subjects at GCE O level. I passed them all, not with flying colours, I might add. I passed well in English, History and Geography, moderately well in French and Biology and scraped through Maths. I wanted to sit A levels with a view to going to drama school or university, but fate or finance decreed otherwise. Grants were much harder to get when I was at school and my family weren't overburdened with £sd. I was only 15 when I sat my exams and too young to leave school anyway. My father settled on the other side of London so I was taken away from St Joseph's during the summer holidays and entered Wallington County Grammar School for a year. I didn't enjoy that year. I missed the nuns and the individual treatment we'd all received. However, scholastically, Wallington was an excellent establishment and from there I went on to do a secretarial course at Ewell Technical College. Daddy and I still argue to this day over how I came to get a secretarial training. He maintains that he didn't know I wanted to act or go to university and I firmly state that he pushed me into technical college. Be that as it may, I couldn't have had a better training for the work I was to do a little later in life.

Work

In 1959 I left Ewell County Technical College with two more O levels in German and Economics, a Certificate from the Royal Society of Arts to say that I was proficient in the Principles of Accounts, Commerce and Shorthand-typewriting. How on earth I ever passed Accounts and Commerce, I'll never know. My present system of accounts is that when the books don't balance I borrow money from my savings to even things up again...sort of robbing Peter to pay Paul. When I left college, fortunately I had a job to go to. Having been thwarted in my theatrical ambitions, I decided the next best thing was to get as close as possible to an affiliated industry. I applied to join the BBC. I took a test, passed and, as I have already mentioned, was offered a job in the Programme

14

Correspondence Section.

If my memory serves me correctly, my starting salary was £6.10s—£2.10s went on my keep at home, another £1.10s on train fares and the remainder served to pay for lunches, clothes and entertainment. I was so proud of being part of that vast organisation affectionately known as 'Auntie' by most who work for her. I very soon joined the Studio Amateur Dramatic Group and the Sailing Club, worked hard and was thrilled to bits whenever I saw anyone famous in the corridors.

The BBC has an excellent reputation for its in-service training schemes and attachments. At that time one of their training establishments was in Marylebone Road, almost opposite Baker Street Tube Station. The building has gone now and has been replaced with yet another soulless multi-storey edifice. Anyway, I had to attend a course there and remember the rickety old lift which bounced up and down several times before it finally came to a halt on the appropriate floor. It was a slow process using that lift, and one day when I was in danger of being late for a lecture I decided my own two feet were quicker and went haring up the stairs only to butt head-first into an extremely tall gentleman. As I raised my eyes to apologise, I went weak at the knees. I was gazing at that wonderful coloured singer, the late Paul Robeson. I blurted my apology and can still see his lovely smile and hear his beautiful voice as he excused me. That was my first *contact*, one might say, with the famous!

Being an ambitious creature, I didn't stay in PCS too long. I applied for and got the job of Junior Secretary in the Science Unit with offices just to the left of the clock on Broadcasting House. I mention the offices because every time I walk into the building I'm reminded of where it all started for me.

The Science Unit consisted of a Senior Producer, a wonderful, quietly-spoken Aberdonian, Dr Archie Clow; a junior producer, mad on the scouting movement, Dr David Edge; a senior secretary who had a love-hate relationship with a Lambretta scooter; and a junior secretary—yours truly. In those days our regular output was a scientific quiz called *Who Knows?* and the two programmes *Science Survey* and *Science Review*. We also did extremely erudite one-off programmes, so technical and high-flown that I hardly knew what I was typing as I pounded away at the scripts. As speakers, we had the top men of the scientific world. I think it was meeting and mixing with such eminent scientific gentlemen at an early age which gave me the apparent poise I used to such good advantage later on in my professional life. After Caroline, the senior secretary, left the Unit, I stepped into her shoes and found myself accompanying Dr Clow to gatherings such as the Annual Meeting of the British Association for the Advancement of Science. Initially I was petrified—how was little Janet Atkins—who wasn't very good at science anyway and had failed Chemistry miserably—how was I going to keep face with all these learned men? But I soon learned that though they were experts in their subjects, they were kindly people and not averse to a chat about the world of entertainment with a very young secretary. I was very happy for those three years with Dr Clow. I worked hard during the day and had an extremely full social life. I had joined an amateur theatrical group called 'The Harlequins' at Wallington in Surrey and spent all my spare time there or at the local youth club attached to St Mary's Church, Beddington.

New Zealand

Then in 1962 came the decision which was eventually to change my whole way of life. I arranged to go to New Zealand with a friend, and left England just as one of the coldest winters on record was about to grasp the country in its icy tentacles.

The Land of the 'Long White Cloud', which is a translation of the Maori name for New Zealand is one of the most beautiful countries I have ever seen. It is said that within the two islands which comprise New Zealand you will find an example of every kind of scenery in the world...mountains, deserts, glaciers, thermal regions, fjords. The New Zealanders are basically friendly, uncomplicated and helpful. I think these were the factors which contributed to my start in television. I simply rang up the head of the New Zealand Broadcasting Commission (NZBC) in Wellington and asked for an appointment, which was granted. I can just imagine trying to do that in England!

I must have been a good talker because all I had to my credit were reams of certificates for Poetry speaking and Drama, a fair amount of *amateur* theatrical experience and a great deal of enthusiasm. I was given a try-out doing Presentation for Television on Sunday evenings. I think my fee was £5. Such riches had to be supplemented by clerical work during the week but it was *experience* and that's something money can't buy. I also did the odd bit of Radio drama for the NZBC and some amateur theatre. I was a long way from any goals at all but I was learning. It was at this time that I changed my name, by deed poll, to 'Leeming'. Janet Leeming sounded theatrically better than my original name and became 'Jan' in Australia where they'll abbreviate even the shortest name.

Australia

After a year I decided to leave New Zealand. Television was very much in its infancy and I couldn't see too many prospects for myself. Also I had two boyfriends and couldn't choose between them so I decided the easiest thing to do was 'run'...but where! I couldn't go back to England because I didn't have enough money. Eventually I went down to Lambton Quay in Wellington, walked into the shipping office and asked where I could go for £35. I was politely informed that my only port of call for that paltry sum would be Sydney, Australia. 'Right', said I, and booked my passage there and then. When I think of it now I shudder.

My arrival in Australia was auspicious, to me at least....As I stepped ashore at Wooloomooloo Quay, a customs officer said in broad Aussie 'D'ye mind if I look at yer bags Miss Hepburn'—Audrey , not Katherine, though I adore them both. Even now, people occasionally suggest that I bear a resemblance to Audrey Hepburn and I literally glow with pride as she's always been a favourite of mine. I quickly returned to earth and realized that I had only £10 in my wallet and the 'phone number of a friend of a friend. I invested in a 'phone call and at least got myself a bed for a few days. I stayed with Darlene Johnson, an actress who's now over here in England and her husband, Bob Moore, who worked for the ABC (Australian Broadcasting Commission) and was an interviewer on a Current Affairs programme called 'Four Corners'...a programme on which Michael Charlton also used to work. He, of course, is now over here and firmly entrenched in Current Affairs programmes for the BBC.

Between Darlene and Bob, I was given good advice as to who I should contact in broadcasting and theatre, but while I was waiting for my letters and 'phone calls to bear fruit, I had to earn a crust. Once again I fell back on my secretarial skills and did temporary work. After nearly two months I found myself working in a solicitor's office, liked the work and was tempted to take the permanent position offered to me. Then I was asked to audition for the ABC who were looking for Television Continuity Announcers. You see, even my moderate experience in New Zealand stood me in good stead. Well, I got the job, or rather three of us did. We were to share Continuity Presentation on Sunday nights. In other words we worked one in three Sundays for the magnificent fee of £10...at least it was a hundred per cent increase on New Zealand! And on the same day, would you believe, I was also offered an acting job with the Young Elizabethans touring the State of New South Wales with potted versions of Shakespearean plays. I couldn't live on £10 every third week but I did want to work for the ABC so eventually a compromise was worked out. My Sunday nights would be fitted in to my touring schedule.

The tour was tough and when it was over I found myself in Sydney again, jobless and overweight! So I took myself off to the beach every day for a few weeks on a diet of fresh fruit and swimming.

Then followed a few months of bits and pieces—a part in a Melbourne-produced television series 'Homicide'; some radio work and the odd commercial. I began to think it would be back to the typewriter for me, when I landed a plum part in a farce called *Diplomatic Baggage* starring Jack Watling.

We opened in Pitt Street in a heat wave in a lovely old but un-air-conditioned theatre called 'The Palace'. Everyone was expiring by the end of the first act...the audience as well as the actors. Suffice it to say, we lasted a week and the curtain came down. There I was once again wondering what to do to pay the rent when I received an offer from one of the commercial channels in Sydney—Channel Ten-10—to become their first woman news-reader. By this time I was only doing my once-every-three weeks stint on the ABC so I decided to accept the news job, which was slightly more permanent...it offered two days employment per week! I'm fortunate in that I've always been extremely good at sight reading and I do have an authoritative voice. I was breaking new ground in a traditionally male orientated society and I succeeded. I was accepted by the public, and received excellent press.

Strangely enough, it was while I was reading news that Robin Bailey saw me on television and asked to meet me. Robin (probably best known to you as Uncle Mort from the BBC TV series *I Didn't Know You Cared* had come out to direct and star in a play by Iris Murdoch called *A Severed Head*. He auditioned me for the juvenile lead in the play...quite a large part really. I think I was only off the stage for one scene. Well, I got the job and I'm glad to say that *A Severed Head* did not suffer the same fate as *Baggage*—in fact it was an unqualified success.

When I look back on it, those four years in New Zealand and Australia were the closest I've ever come to a charmed existence. The Gods really did seem to be smiling on me.

A Severed Head ran in Sydney for several months and then went on tour to Melbourne, Newcastle and Canberra. All in all we played for about seven months. During this time I was also continuing my newsreading on Channel Ten-10 on Sunday nights and indeed when we went down to Melbourne, the company paid for me to commute by plane to fulfill my newsreading duties. But all good things come to an end—they had a change of policy and my dual life of actress/newsreader was over. In fact, when I first went to Ten, part of the carrot dangled was to use me as an interviewer but this never materialized.

Next came a short run in a David Turner comedy, *Semi-Detached* and hardly enough time to worry about being out of work, when an offer came to join the Union Theatre Repertory Company in Melbourne. I was not too happy to leave my beloved Sydney but the Union Rep had a high reputation and could do nothing but benefit my career. It was a good season for me and I landed several plum parts, the most coveted of which was the role of Natasha (shades of Audrey Hepburn in *War and Peace*). That role was sheer unadulterated magic...I almost lived the part.

You may be wondering why, in a book about a career in television, I've spent so much time talking about my relatively short theatrical career. You will find that many presenters on television have been in theatre or have dabbled with it in an amateur capacity. Because even though it's you, in the role of *yourself*, on the box, it's still a dramatic performance. Most of us are subject to the same nervous tension when doing a programme as is felt before a curtain rises. And the same training which gives an actor/actress that important quality of 'stillness' and command in the theatre is brought to bear in a television performance. I'm not suggesting for one moment that you *must* have a theatrical training—indeed some of our finest presenters haven't been near a stage—but in my particular case the experience was invaluable.

Being with the Union Rep was almost the closing chapter of my life as an actress. In July 1966 I turned my thoughts homewards and booked a passage immediately after the rep season had finished.

As was my wont, I arrived home with hardly a penny to my name. I spent a few weeks seeing old friends and then turned my mind to the hard business of finding work. With 'rave notices' for my theatrical performances in Austrialia and introductions from Robin Bailey and Jack Watling to some influential people in London, I thought it was only a question of some 'phone calls and pavement pounding before Londoners realized what a talent they had in their midst! Reality hit hard. My experience in Australia appeared to count for nothing and interviews were difficult to arrange. Back to the drawing board. I took temporary secretarial work again, to keep the wolf from the door. I am a good and efficient secretary and, as had happened in the past, several of the people for whom I worked on a temporary basis tried to tempt me into a full time post. I almost succumbed, when at the eleventh hour I was offered a contract. Auditions were being held at the London offices of Granada

Television for a female television presenter and newsreader. I still remember walking into the waiting room and seeing a staggeringly attractive woman whom I discovered was Sara Leighton, a well-known painter. I practically walked out there and then being quite sure that she would get the job. Perhaps she'd had no television experience because it was little old me who got offered a four-day week, six-month contract to work in Manchester. I must say that after the sublime climate of Australia and being an ignorant southerner anyway, the thought of Manchester in the winter time did nothing at all to warm the cockles of my heart, but a job is a job and one has to go where the work is.

I was to travel up to Manchester on a Monday morning, work through till Thursday and return by train that evening. For the first week, I was booked into a pub/hotel quite close to the Granada studios. Ironically, it was called 'The New Inn' though it was as old as the hills and grotty, but had a great deal of atmosphere as well as no locks on the bedroom doors. It was a meeting place for many of the Granada lot—I don't know where they go now it's been pulled down and given way to a modern complex. There were few mod cons but they served a smashing breakfast if you didn't mind the smell of stale beer—we had to eat in what was the bar the night before. I found myself facing, over breakfast, quite a few well known actors who'd also been booked into the pub, while making plays for Granada.

Several of the folk, who were around the Company for the few months I was there, have done extremely well, professionally, since then. Mike Scott, who was an interviewer on a magazine programme is now the Programme Controller. Bob Grieves, who worked on the News Desk as a Sub, now presents the nightly news programme and reads the news. Vanya Kewley is doing prestigious documentary programmes and is a fine interviewer. I don't know what would have happened to me if I hadn't panicked. Let me explain—basically, in broadcasting, no news is good news in that if no-one criticises your work then you can normally rest assured that you're doing all right. Granada were very good to me, even going so far as to send me out with the wardrobe mistress to buy some after-six dresses in which to read the news. They were, of course, the company's property but I had full access to them. Funnily enough, several years later I saw an actress wearing a very distinctive black number in a play. It was originally bought for me!

I obviously couldn't stay at The New Inn for too long so I asked around about cheapish accommodation and was recommended to a Mrs Hoey who ran theatrical digs. It was a really homely establishment and a motley crowd of people, actors and television folk would stay there, often chatting into the wee small hours. One Monday, I'd come straight up from London and gone to work at the studios then off to Mrs Hoey's in the evening. I must have had a meal and stayed chatting late because when I went up to my bedroom it was already occupied by a rather large gentleman of the acting fraternity who was in a very sound sleep laced, I think, with a touch of the hard stuff. I couldn't wake him nor move him, so I had to spend the night in a rather cold attic bedroom. Apparently this gentleman often stayed at Mrs H's and automatically went to the same room he'd always had, without checking with her first. It was quite amusing at the time. After Mrs Hoey's I joined forces with a lovely lass called Sue Michison, who was a Production Assistant, and we rented a cottage from Pat Phoenix of *Coronation Street*. Sue is now a married lady with three children and still a very close friend.

I received favourable press while in Manchester but my six months were drawing to a close and no-one had mentioned an extension of contract. So when my agent 'phoned and suggested that I attend an audition in London, I went. The job on offer was that of a Presentation Announcer for Westward Television in Plymouth. I was successful and the position was mine if I wanted it.

By this time I was feeling restricted by the job I was doing and wanted to branch out into interviewing so I made noises in that direction to the Westward people. They agreed that I might be able to 'spread my wings' a trifle once I was with them. My agent signed the contract on my behalf and I went to the Granada bosses to thank them for having me and to tell them I was off. They were most surprised. Apparently I was supposed to have realized that my contract would have been renewed. Anyway, the deed was done and I was obliged to leave. I've often fantasized and imagined that if I'd stayed in Manchester I might have ended up presenting an excellent programme like the magazine programme 'Cinema'. However, it's pointless to look back at what might have been.

I'd saved a little money by this time and decided that I would like to have a car. I bought a soft-top 'frog-eyed' Sprite for a sum in the region of £300, on HP of course. I was so proud of it when I brought it to my mother's home in Windsor. I was to set off next day for Plymouth. In the morning, I packed the car, said goodbye to everyone, including my black miniature poodle Sheba, and the first port of call was a garage to check oil, tyre pressures and fill up with petrol. I didn't reach Plymouth. At approximately 2.30 in the afternoon I was driving towards Salisbury on the old Roman road at a speed of around 45 mph. Suddenly the car zigzagged out of control and I saw the small saplings at the side of the road coming towards me. All hell semed to be let loose and the next thing was comparative calm and me trapped underneath the vehicle. I remember thinking 'Dear God don't let the car catch fire'—it was almost a year previously that my fiancé had died in a crash and that thought was uppermost in my mind. I was very fortunate because the driver of a car travelling in the opposite direction had seen the accident and came back immediately. He and a friend managed to pull the car off me. I don't remember being in any pain but I couldn't see too well. I panicked and was assured that my eyes were alright but that I'd a bad gash on my nose and it was the blood from that wound which was causing the temporary blindness. The ambulancemen appeared on the scene remarkably quickly and I was taken to Salisbury General Hospital, where they sewed up my various cuts. It was the nose which bothered them. I was X-rayed and it was discovered that I'd a compound fracture. Fortunately for me, we were practically on the doorstep of Odstock Hospital which specializes in burns and plastic surgery. Again the Gods smiled, for when the call was put out, the only man available to come and look at the wreckage—me—was the senior plastic surgeon, a kind man and marvellous at his work, Mr John Barron. To cut a long story short, I went into surgery round about midnight and came out with such small stitches in my facial wounds that I reckon he'd have won a prize for needlework. The nose had swollen too much to have anything other than a splint put on it. It's strange but, at a time like that, you don't think of your damages, you're just so glad to be alive. The nurses wouldn't let me have a mirror for days and when I finally got my hands on one I felt a moment of despair. My whole face was swollen and very bruised, one eyelid had been sewn up, they'd had to 'sand' one side of my face to get out the gravel and glass and I had a tin splint on my nose. 'That's it' I thought, 'I'll never appear on camera again. But I did and quite quickly too. While in Odstock, I was completely bowled over by the kindness of people I'd never met. Westward TV had given my arrival a good deal of publicity so when I didn't make it, I received flowers, fruit, letters and get well cards in abundance, from viewers in the Plymouth area. Because of the wonders of make-up, I was actually able to go back on screen within a month. That wasn't the end of the matter though. I had damaged my nose and caused a bump near the bridge so Mr Barron suggested that I come back to Odstock in about three months time and have it seen to. I still remember him coming up to my bed and asking what kind of a nose I wanted. 'I've always wanted a retroussé nose'—'Well, that wouldn't suit your bone structure' said the surgeon and promptly picked up a copy of *'Vanity Fair'*—a magazine I'd been reading. He flipped through it and pointed to a picture of a good looking model—'that's the sort of bone structure you've got, how about that one?' And that's what I ended up with—a rather attractive nose which in many respects is better than the one I was born with.

My year at Westward was pleasant and uneventful. It was pleasant because you find that in a region people become attached to their local 'personalities'. They write to you with their problems, tell you about their families, ask you to attend fêtes and functions and generally 'love' you. As a Presentation Announcer, you work odd shifts. Westward was no exception. The working hours were not conducive to a social life and I only had one weekend in three off which usually saw me belting back to the big smoke in my newly acquired Triumph Spitfire.

One usually finds that the people in a small TV station are very friendly and there's a good feeling of camaraderie. Westward was no exception and I had many a good chat and laugh with the technical boys when I was on a late duty. One of the most amusing events of that year now that I look back at it was the Christmas pantomime, *Cinderella*. It wasn't quite such fun at the time! I was chosen to be Cinders and various 'on-camera' personalities played the other roles. The only problem was that some bright spark suggested that we did it on location as a film. Ha! Ha! There I was dressed in the skimpiest of tatty rags trying to be a lovely Cinderella as I was turning blue with cold. It had snowed the night before! One thing about filming—the show goes on whatever the weather. Unfortunately I never did see the end result because I had a few days leave at the time it was transmitted and had done my usual disappearing act back to my mother's home in Windsor.

I suppose I've always been ambitious and, despite the pleasantness of my job, I felt frustrated. For many reasons my opportunity for interviewing never came to fruition so at the end of my year's contract I decided to leave. Fool that I was—I walked straight into unemployment again. This time I wasn't out of work long enough to contemplate the typewriter and shorthand notebook. I had a 'phone call from Lewis Fiander, an actor I'd met in Australia. He was doing a season at the Oxford Playhouse and one of the bit-part players had fallen ill. As the company were already well into rehearsal and Frank Hauser didn't want the hassle of auditions, he took Lewis's word as to my acting ability and hired me for a short season. So there I was, quite unexpectedly, back on the 'boards' again. The parts were small—one of the court ladies,

23

with a few sentences to utter, in Ben Jonson's *Epicoene* (*The Silent Woman*) and at the other extreme—a street girl with a sonnet-and-a-bit in Robert Browning's verse play *Pippa Passes*. There were some very talented people in that company—the beautiful Stephanie Beauchamp who has since done very well in films; good looking Tony Anholt, who does a good deal of television work, and who appeared with the fabulous Alexandra Bastedo in a long running series; Phillip Voss who has a magnificent voice and is often to be heard in radio plays—just to mention a few. Those three months were quite fun but I can't say the parts were rewarding and I didn't like living in digs. I'm a great home lover. Wanting to be in one's own home and in the entertainment business are mutually exclusive desires. Even the most renowned stars have to spend a great deal of time away from home, although they probably stay in decent hotels and not cold digs. I think, too, that I was beginning to realize that I was temperamentally unsuited to the see-saw of being in and out of work and literally living to hear the telephone ring with an offer of work. I'm not suggesting that television is as 'safe as houses'—far from it—but you do have the opportunity of signing contracts for a six month to two-year period which is about as much security as you'll ever get.

The Oxford Playhouse season came to an end and we all kissed and promised to keep in touch—which we didn't. It's so difficult to maintain friendships when you disperse in different directions and move on to alternative projects.

So there I was again—unemployed. Then out of the blue I received a 'phone call from Tom Salmon who was Head of the BBC in Plymouth dealing with the South West Region. He was desperate for a Television Presentation Announcer—would I take the job? Also Angela Rippon was about to leave them to go to Westward Television. I didn't really want to be confined to announcing and newsreading again so we struck a compromise. I would take the job and Tom would allow and generally encourage me to do interviewing. Promises are often broken in business generally but I'm delighted to say that Tom honoured his word and it's him more than anyone that I have to thank for putting my feet on the path in the direction I wanted to go. I must say it was a rather odd situation for Angela to have left the Beeb for Westward and for me to have left Westward and be joining the BBC. Normally, years would have to elapse before an 'on camera' person would be tolerated working for the opposition in the same region.

I shall never forget my first interview assignment. It was an interview with a shantyman (a singer of songs of the sea) for

24

inclusion in a morning radio programme, now defunct, called 'Today in the South and West' (nicknamed TISWAS although I never quite knew why). I duly trotted off with my recording machine. Stan Hugill was such an engaging man that we happily chattered on for an hour and I used up four reels of tape. That was fine until I came back to base.

There's such a thing in broadcasting as recording to a ratio for both radio and television. This means that you obviously record more than you need in order to be able to cut the item into a cohesive whole but somehow this vital piece of information hadn't been communicated to me. The average ratio, although of course individuals differ, is a maximum of about seven to one in television and three to one in radio. I had recorded sixty minutes worth for a two minute item. I simply didn't know where to start with the editing. I can still see Tom Salmon at his desk, myself near to tears, saying that this time he'd edit the tape for me but woe betide me if I ever came back with that amount of tape again. I never did. I don't think it is essential to do radio interviews before working in television but it certainly helps and teaches you discipline. I learnt very quickly. For a two-minute item you must be precise. The basic rule is to work out a rough order of questions and stick to them unless your interviewee goes up a side road that is so interesting, you are forced to follow. I'm not suggesting for one minute that you should stick rigidly to your questions regardless of the answers but you must always be aware of the shape of an interview. It must have a beginning, middle and end—a scene set, substance and some kind of finale, even if not conclusion. You have to judge your guest and always make allowances for nervousness. Very often it will pay you, as the interviewer, to scene set and give the outline of the story; otherwise, trying to elicit the same information from a guest could use up your valuable interviewing time.

I remained at BBC Plymouth for almost a year. My basic job was to do television presentation which meant being at the station, mainly in the evenings, and doing the announcements in-between programmes. This was not quite as simple as it sounds. The BBC regions take a large number of the programmes originating from the Network in London but from time to time they 'opt-out' to do their own thing. Therefore, the announcer has to be able to hear what's going on in London, by means of an earpiece, and to take timings accordingly. It's like trying to rub your stomach and pat your head at the same time.

While I was at Plymouth, their local news magazine programme was presented by Hugh Scully (now on *Nationwide*) and Sheila

25

Tracey (now on BBC Radio 2). Angela Rippon and Sue Lawley also launched forth from Plymouth and any success I've had must be laid at Tom Salmon's doorstep. I think Tom really enjoyed seeing his fledglings succeed. It was he who suggested that I should audition for a Network Children's programme called *Tom-Tom*. I hadn't even heard of the impending auditions, but Tom had and he pushed me in the right direction. Let me explain that not all the Network programmes are produced in London. It would be almost a physical impossibility. So, certain programmes, although networked from Lands End to John O' Groats, are produced in regions. *Tom-Tom* had its base in Bristol. It was a sort of junior *Tomorrow's World* and was presented by John Earle and Norman Tozer. The producer was an extremely bright Oxbridge graduate called Richard Wade and he'd made the decision that the programme needed a female presenter. I was accepted and duly presented myself for an audition. It's one of the few auditions I actually remember. Perhaps because I thought I had a cheek, with my non-scientific background, to even be considering myself as a candidate. We had to explain a complicated piece of equipment in simple terms, talk about an odd-shaped piece of wood with a hole in and try and assess what it was and also give a two to three minute talk to camera on a subject of our own choosing. I decided to recount my experience on an Opal field in Australia and lapsed into the vernacular where necessary. I don't know if that's what clinched it but years later the producer told me what an impression I'd made with that little talk. Anyway, the job was mine if I wanted it. I can't think there are many broadcasters who don't finally aim at working for Network Television. Needless to say, I took the thirteen week contract and moved up to Bristol. First problem was to find accommodation. That's a thankless task anywhere but Bristol is a University city and I arrived just after the start of the autumn session, so there was no cheap accommodation to be had. It was 1969 and £15 a week was a great deal to pay in rent then but that's what I ended up doing. Mind you, looking back now £15 a week for a whole house seems ludicrous. I touted round the BBC and found a girl who also needed a roof over her head and we decided to share.

I can still remember the feeling of euphoria when I went up to Television Centre (Mecca to me) for publicity photographs. I also remember thinking that this was my 'open sesame' and that I'd probably travel the world like Val Singleton who was on the children's programme *Blue Peter* at the time. Suffice it to say that the furthest I ever travelled for *Tom-Tom* was the beautiful city of Norwich. I may not have become part of the jet-set but I learned a great deal from that programme. To start with, a large proportion of the items were of the demonstration variety—explaining how a gadget worked or interviewing an expert who would do the explanations. In the latter type of interview your job was to ensure that the expert explained succinctly—a difficult task with many boffins who do not understand 'simplicity'. My colleagues on the show were John Earle—I wonder if he's still an inveterate mountain climber—and Norman Tozer whose name I still occasionally see in the *Radio Times*.

You will find that most series on television run for a quarter—thirteen weeks—take a break and then come back again. Well, in the breaks you have to earn a living and I was fortunate enough to be able to do radio interviewing for *Today in the South and West* to which I'd previously contributed from Plymouth. This work kept me ticking over until the new series of *Tom-Tom*. Under the guidance of radio producers Brian Skilton and Jonathan Fulford, both of whom I was to work with later, I think my radio interviewing improved and this in turn affected my television work.

After the second *Tom-Tom* run, I found myself once again scraping round for a living until the programme's return in the Autumn. It was while engaged on a radio interview during this period that mini disaster struck. I'd been sent to do a story on a farm far south of Bristol. When I arrived the farmer refused to speak to me—a not uncommon occurrence when one's engaged in the interviewing business. Anyway, I was half way to Cornwall and it was a Friday, so I made a quick decision to keep on going. My boyfriend lived in St Austell and we got so little opportunity to see each other that this seemed like a God-sent situation. His parents were, and still are, very dear friends and I knew they'd accommodate me. I had a lovely weekend and then received a 'phone call from my flat-mate, Claire, informing me that she too was visiting Cornwall and would I mind picking her up and taking her back to Bristol with me when I returned. I shall never know whether it was those extra misty and difficult miles added to my journey which tired me but when we were sixteen miles from Bristol I took a corner, went into a skid and ended up saying hello to a telegraph pole. When we came to a standstill I remember doing a spot check—Claire was all right, Sheba was OK, and so was I, or was I? As I clambered out of the car and put my right foot on to the ground I collapsed in a heap in terrible pain. I hadn't realised that the driver's side of the car had been pushed towards the centre on impact and my leg had been in the way. I was taken to Weston Super Mare General Hospital with a broken leg and fractured ankle. I can still remember the pain. Because the broken bone had lacerated my leg, the surgeon was unable to put on a plaster. The wound had to be given time to heal but the ankle couldn't be left without plaster for too long or it would have set incorrectly. While I was in hospital I received the bill from the Council for the telegraph pole! And another bombshell — a letter from Monica Sims, the Assistant Head of Children's Programmes, informed me that *Tom-Tom* was to be axed after the Autumn series. Miss Sims thanked me for my work and hoped that I'd enjoy working on the last series. So there I was with half a leg in plaster, the threat of a permanent limp hanging over me, and incapable of work, not to mention a written-off car. 'Never mind, I'll muddle through somehow until the programme starts again' I thought. But even that wasn't to be. Our Programme Editor, Richard Wade, who'd initially hired me, was elevated to the position of Editor, *Tomorrow's World* and off he went. The chap who took the programme over decided to make changes and I was one of them. So there I was 'unemployed' again at a time when I couldn't have felt lower. Because I was under contract, the BBC honoured it's financial obligation to me but nothing is worse than being out of work even if you are being paid. Mind you, they say that behind every cloud there's a silver lining and events were about to take a powerful turn for the better. My leg healed and fortunately I didn't limp, although I do have one leg fractionally shorter than the other. I moved out of my rented house and into a very much cheaper flat which I shared with an extremely nice girl. Then out of the blue I was asked to audition as a presenter for a new women's programme about to be launched on HTV West — that's the commercial television channel in Bristol. It was by way of an experiment and the programme was to run for *eight weeks*. I got the job and the programme ran for *eight years* with me working on it for six of them.

In a nutshell, I was expected to go into the studio in Bath Road for a day's research and to be briefed on the programme in general and the next day we recorded two programmes. Back at the end of 1969 when *Women Only* started it was only twelve minutes long but by the time I left the programme, mid '76, it was just short of half an hour.

The director was Mike Towers who now holds the post of Production Controller and the researcher was Jill Roach, a highly gifted young lady who is now a Senior Producer with the BBC responsible for *John Craven's Newsround* (see page 55). In the beginning we were all determined to avoid cooking, craft and the usual format that goes into so many women's programmes. But that seemed to be what the audience wanted so that's what they got plus book reviews, the odd interview with a star—not too many make their way to the West Country and those that do often don't have time to visit the studio. Whatever its drawbacks, the programme obviously fulfilled some kind of need and it just went on. I think it improved and strengthened over the years as should any programme that's allowed to establish itself. It's only a personal view but I often think that companies don't give programmes enough time to iron out the creases before they are axed. Anyway, fortunately, and for whatever reason, we just kept running. I enjoyed the programme tremendously—it was my baby and I hope I did my fair share of nursing it along. I know it gave me the opportunity to improve my television presentation and my interviewing technique.

I was working two days a week and just about earning enough on which to live when Ron Evans, the Editor of HTV's nightly news magazine programme, asked me if I would be free to do the odd film story for his programme. I was delighted to accept and by early 1970 found myself working a couple of days for *Report West* and another couple for *Women Only*. This was all on freelance and ad hoc basis so that when I was asked to sign a year's contract with the company, I acquiesced very happily. Mind you, I nearly came unstuck before I started. I had, of course, had experience of filming at the BBC in Plymouth but was unfamiliar with the technique of recording interviews for a news programme.

I remember it well because Tony Holmes (who is now Editor of *Report West*) accompanied me on my first interview for safety's sake and just as well too! I can't remember the details of the story but it was something to do with travel and air hostesses and the venue was the Royal Hotel in Bristol. I'd worked out my basic questioning and was feeling reasonably relaxed. The camera started to roll and the interview went ahead quite smoothly. Flushed with pride I turned to Tony who said 'Great, now we'll do some cutaways'—What on earth were they? Cutaways are actually the interviewer's questions recorded on film separately. They are also known as 'reverses'. They are used to facilitate editing later. The film editor can cut short an answer and drop in the next question. Tony had anticipated my omitting to write out my questions and had actually taken them down as I asked them. The day was saved! I get the feeling that you can never know all there is to be known about broadcasting—you're always learning something new.

Round about that time ITN introduced its system of having two newsreaders to present the *News at Ten*. Ron Evans thought this might be a good idea for *Report West* and teamed me up with the programme's main presenter Bruce Hockin. It worked and the audience liked the idea of a man and women presenting the programme together. It was like a mini Golden Age for me. I thoroughly enjoyed working with Bruce and the *Report West* team in general. I had and still have the greatest respect for Ron Evans. He was an excellent News Editor who knew just what he wanted from his programme and got it with the minimum of fuss and aggravation. Ron was also very good at dealing with his team which is a lot more than I can say for many people in the broadcasting and theatrical field. I always feel that a please and thank you will get you further ahead than shouting, yet our industry seems to breed shouters.

I've always said that when you work on television in a reasonably small region, people become very attached to you and if you're not careful you end up with never a weekend to call your own—always out opening some fête or bazaar or some such function. Don't misunderstand, I thoroughly enjoyed it all but there were times when I longed for a bit of privacy. I do sympathize with the very well known personalities, because having experienced a little of it myself, I realize how public your life becomes.

People don't seem to realize how very much preparation goes into television and radio programmes. I was constantly asked what I did with myself all day as I only appeared on television for half an hour each night. There are interviews to be filmed, returned to the studio for developing, scripting and editing into a form suitable for transmission. Studio interviews have to be rehearsed—scripts to be checked through—and a visit to make-up must be fitted in. What a bind that was when I was trying to grow my hair. In the early days with *Report West* I used to go out filming, dash back to base, try and organize my script and also hope that Val or Chris the make-up girls would work a miracle with my hair. In the end I declared myself beaten and have kept my hair in a short, straight urchin cut for years just so that I would look tidy on camera whatever the weather.

Women Only was a recorded studio programme and we usually did two in a day. I'd arrive about 9.30 for rehearsal at 10.00. There would be three to four interviews contained within the programme and these would be rehearsed during the course of the morning. At about 12.00 noon we'd break for camera 'line-up' where all the cameras are trained on to a test card to ascertain that they are putting out a perfect picture. About 12.30 we'd record and hope that we'd get it all 'in the can' in one take. Of course, if something went drastically wrong, then we would stop recording and start again from a suitable point but on a low budget programme such as

Women Only there wasn't much leeway for mistakes. Then we'd have lunch and repeat the process in the afternoon, finishing around 4.30 in time to get me into Studio B (a smaller news studio) for *Report West* rehearsal.

Over six years it was very interesting to watch the changes in *Women Only*. To begin with it was only transmitted in the HTV West region. Then gradually it was taken by more of the independent stations until it was going out in the Southern region, Yorkshire, Tyne Tees, Border and Anglia. Jill Roach, our researcher, left to join the BBC and Barbara Twigg took over. Barbara had worked for a longish period for Randolph Churchill and was very much into books and authors. *Women Only* changed subtly and in a way that I particularly liked. I've always most enjoyed interviewing people from the world of entertainment or authors and now the programme contained one or two book reviews each week. I didn't always get the book item but was delighted when it came my way. It was a long time before I could pluck up the courage to ask the various guests to autograph their books for me and I'm very sorry for this omission because the autographed copies on my bookshelves afford me a great deal of pleasurable reminiscence. I look at Mary Chipperfield's books and remember going to her home where she was surrounded by all manner of four-footed friends, including a black panther. I interviewed Noel Barber, brother of ex-Chancellor of the Exchequer, Anthony Barber, during Wimbledon season. I remember him arriving in a red gingham shirt, plus trousers and jacket of course, puffing at a cigar and being so entertaining. On that occasion his book was *Lords of the Golden Horn*, the story of the fall of the Ottoman Empire. I've always been fascinated by historical books and this one was enthralling.

Another character I remember was George Melly, the blues and jazz singer and critic. He was a delightful chap to interview. If you know of him you'll remember that he usually wears 1920s 'prohibition style' suits in very loud stripes bearing a close relationship to deck chair material. I asked him why he wore such attire and he replied quite reasonably that he liked the gear and added that he was always careful not to sit down on a bench at the seaside in case someone actually paid for a ticket and sat on him!

Nicolette Milnes Walker is a petite, pretty and feminine lady who, in the Summer of 1971 crossed the Atlantic single handed. She wrote a book on her exploits about which I was fortunate enough to talk to her for *Women Only*. That infectious lady Margaret Powell paid a couple of visits to the programme and had every one in stitches. She entered domestic service at the age of 15, married and had three sons, all of whom went to university and then Margaret herself returned to her own education at the age of 58. Her first book *Below Stairs* published in 1968 launched her on a career as a writer, lecturer and broadcaster and she's continued to write very amusingly about her years 'in service'. Jackie Collins, Joan's sister, came down to HTV when her book *Lovehead* was published. What a beautiful and pleasant woman she is! During the *Women Only* days I think the author who impressed me most as a person was that lovely lady, actress Nanette Newman.

It wasn't all moonlight and roses though. One would get difficult guests—difficult for a variety of reasons—nervous of the cameras, unable to communicate clearly or just someone with whom one felt no empathy. Happily, these occasions were in the minority. Sometimes I'd find that I just couldn't get the interview off to a good start. I remember interviewing the late Stanley Baker. He was charming but I was rather over-awed by him and just couldn't get the interview together.

Sometimes we'd concentrate the whole programme on one subject. I was able to persuade Barbara to look at the work of the delightful fashion designer Gina Fratini. Gina loathes synthetic fabrics and tends to use, unfortunately for one's pocket, beautiful silks and chiffons. Barbara conceived the idea of doing a programme about silk from the cocoon upwards and ending with an interview with Gina and a mini fashion parade of swirling gossamer-like Fratini creations.

Barbara left HTV in 1975 and went up to Yorkshire Television where she's been doing some prestigious work on programmes such as *Whicker's World*, and a series with Sir Harold Wilson. *Women Only* changed again with the next researcher Monica Foot. Monica had a strong grounding in the musical world so for a while the programme included interviews with many singing stars and musicians—Barbara Dickson, the group *Sailor*, the composer of *African Sanctus,* David Fanshawe, immediately spring to mind.

They were good and happy years at HTV. I was very much part of a team, enjoyed my work and was well-liked by the public. I belonged. So why did I go and mess it all up? *Ambition*—I suppose. I wanted to become more involved in production but as the powers that be were quite happy with me doing five *Report West* and two *Women Only* programmes a week, they weren't prepared to rock the boat. Anyway, fate intervened.

In February 1976 I was sitting in the make-up department at HTV when I received a call from Glasgow. A girl with the most gentle

Scots accent told me that she was 'phoning on behalf of Mike Marshall of the BBC to ask if I would be interested in being auditioned for a series of documentary programmes on Food. How on earth had they heard of me?! It transpired that the producer had wanted to engage Angela Rippon but she had too many commitments and over a dinner table in Aberdeen he had mentioned his problem. Michael Buerk, an old colleague from HTV who was by then working as the BBC's Industrial Correspondent, suggested yours truly. I went up to Glasgow, did the audition and was offered the job. It was for a series of thirteen programmes and that presented me with a dilemma. If I accepted the BBC offer, I would really be sticking my neck out and afterwards, what then? Once again, compromise was the order of the day. Ron Evans didn't want to lose me so he very kindly agreed to my having a couple of days off each week to do *The Food Programme* in Scotland and the other three I was to continue with *Report West*. I lost *Women Only* though, which was a bit of a blow.

It was a hectic but fun period shuttling up and down to Glasgow each week. I was working with Donny Macleod and Derek Cooper. Derek is a food and wine connoisseur and the programme was predominantly his idea. The whole team was such fun to work with. Derek and Donny are marvellous *raconteurs*. We'd all meet up on a Thursday night with Mike Marshall, the producer, and Jeannie Hodge or Ellie Taylor, his production assistants. Being a programme about food we had to test various restaurants didn't we? I don't think I've ever laughed so much as I did during the three series I did with that motley crew. In the first series, I found myself doing mainly studio interviews and presentation. Towards the end of the run I was in a state of turmoil. What was I going to do? I'm not very brave and adventurous and I really do like to keep the *status quo* but I'd had a taste of doing a programme on a larger scale than HTV offered and didn't know whether I would be able to earn a living as a total freelance. That wasn't the only consideration. I loved living in Bristol — I had my life neatly planned and all my friends around me. I think I would have opted for the comfort and safety of HTV had I not received a 'phone call from the Editor of *Pebble Mill*, a BBC networked lunchtime magazine programme. I must admit that I was flattered when he asked to meet me for lunch. Apparently *Pebble Mill* was one presenter short and Donny Macleod, who worked on the programme, had recommended me to Terry Dobson on the strength of my work for *The Food Programme*.

We had lunch at one of the best restaurants in Bristol, Harveys. Don't run away with the idea that this kind of treat was a regular occurrence. I'm usually offered a job over a cup of coffee if I'm lucky! Terry was offering me a one year contract to commence in the September. The money wasn't very good—roughly the same as I was getting at HTV but the lure of 'Network' television was very strong. Once again I thought it would be the open sesame to a brilliant career. While I was agonizing over my decision and dear Ron Evans was doing his best to persuade me to stay at HTV, I was asked to present a ten week networked series of craft programmes also for the BBC. I think it was that which pushed me into a decision. I really felt that I'd arrived. Nothing could stop me. I hadn't felt that way since my thespian triumphs over a decade before. With tremendous regret I decided to leave HTV. And with hindsight it was a move I've paid for dearly in terms of my personal happiness.

I left *Report West* at the end of June 1976 and started work on *Knitting Fashion* which would keep me in funds up until the time I was to go to Birmingham to join the *Pebble Mill* team. Working on *Knitting Fashion* was a very happy experience. Jenny Rodgers, the producer, was a gem to work for, as was Sheila Innes, the Executive Producer. Pam Dawson, the knitting expert, and I hit it off extremely well.

In fact the whole team including Libby the director and Helen the secretary was a very happy one. Although the series was to go out on the Network, it was recorded in Bristol at the BBC Studios about 500 metres from my home in Clifton.

You may wonder why I stress the fact that both the 'Food Programme' and Knitting Fashion' were happy programmes on which to work. The reason is that television is a time-consuming, often frustrating medium and tempers run high, so that when there's an overall atmosphere of calm, one remembers it well. I recall the floor manager in Bristol, Chris, saying that he couldn't understand it—here we were, a whole team of women working on a programme and it was so harmonious. Why shouln't it be?

The series turned out to be very successful and was repeated constantly. Everyone thought this was marvellous for me but it wasn't really. It sort of works in reverse. If your face is constantly being seen it tends to put producers off the idea of using you because of a danger of over-exposure. I got my last repeat-fee cheque at the beginning of 1979 so in fact the programme had been around for three years.

I forgot to mention that in 1971 I had acquired another dog, a standard poodle bitch called Fleur. I thought my wandering days were over and that I'd probably stay in Bristol permanently, otherwise I certainly wouldn't have taken on the extra responsibility, although I can't imagine life without my doggie companions. When I went up to *Pebble Mill* I couldn't take Fleur and Sheba with me so they went to stay with my mother. I used to motor up to Birmingham on a Monday morning, leaving home at 6.45 am, stay there during the week and belt down the motorway home on Fridays.

Pebble Mill was a very exciting and also very hair-raising programme on which to work. For a start it was predominantly a 'live' show. For those of you who haven't seen it, let me explain. It comes from the reception area of the BBC studios at Pebble Mill in Birmingham. Why from the reception area? Well, when the studios were built, for some reason there was an enormous lobby stretching almost the entire length of the front of the building. Someone decided that it was an awful waste of space and the idea was conceived to erect scaffolding on the ceiling which would be capable of holding studio lights, and then the lobby could be used as an extra studio. Because it is an area not designed as a studio, there are many headaches for the technical people, particularly the lighting men. In a normal studio there are no windows and therefore no daylight so the lighting engineer can draw up a lighting plot knowing that once set it will remain static. With *Pebble Mill* the lights can be set at 10.00 am and by the time the programme goes on the air at 1.00 pm bright sunshine streaming through the glass, or dark clouds, could unbalance everything.

A typical *Pebble Mill* day began at 9 o'clock with a meeting to discuss the contents of the programme and iron out any forseeable difficulties. Guests would start to arrive around 10 am. The researcher who had set up the item would look after them initially and ascertain that they'd brought everything necessary for the interview. Then the presenters would meet their guests and thrash out the format of the interview. We could be called on at any time between 10.30 and 12.30 to take our guests down to the lobby floor for rehearsal. Everyone also had to pay a visit to make-up. My goodness what a job of diplomacy make-up girls have. Quite often women guests would arrive with either totally unsuitable make-up for the television medium or else they'd use none at all, and Jenny, our special make-up artist for the programme, would have to use all her powers of persuasion to assure them that in so far as television cameras were concerned, she knew best!

Clothes are a problem on the screen. The most suitable colours for television are those in what I call the 'autumn' spectrum; harsh blues and reds create problems and certain patterns strobe—giving an impression of busyness and movement. I don't know what came first in my choice of clothing, tent-like dresses to accommodate radio microphones tied round my waist underneath them, or voluminous dresses because I liked them. For Marian Foster and myself, the wearing of necklaces was out of the question because we always had to consider the small microphone pinned on us. A necklace clattering against that would have driven the sound man mad.

If you've seen the programme, you'll know that often we'd be outside for an item and then back inside later. That presented more problems for us women than for the men. If we were outside and it was blowing a gale or raining, how could we appear calm and unruffled ten minutes later in the studio. It was all good fun though and people certainly respond well to the challenge of 'live' television.

We used 'autocue' for our links in between items and often this would be the last thing to be rehearsed in a hectically busy schedule or else wouldn't be rehearsed at all. Many's the time we've all started to read a link only to see the camera disappearing at a rapid rate of knots down the studio to be in its next position. I never went on to the floor of the studio without making sure that my script was somewhere within reach in case of such an emergency. If I were sitting on a stool, very often the only place for it was under my behind but at least if I knew it was there it gave me a degree of confidence.

People are always asking about amusing incidents that have happened and I now wish that I'd kept a little black book in which to jot them all down. But I didn't and I've now forgotten a great many incidents which I thought would be etched on my memory forever. I don't know if it would qualify as amusing, although I suppose in the long run it was—I had to interview four very beautiful Indian women with the most long and difficult names. Realising I'd never remember them, old clever clogs wrote them with a ball point pen, one along each digit of my left hand. During the course of rehearsal, I got hot, sweaty and nervous. You've guessed—when it came to the show, I looked down at a blue smudge. There was nothing for it. I had to own up and ask the women to introduce themselves. *Ad-libbing* is a very valuable gift if you're working as an interviewer/presenter in television or radio. I've had to *ad-lib* my way out of tight corners on more occasions than I can remember. The strange thing is that afterwards I cannot remember what I said. I'm assured that it always made sense.

David Seymour, a very fine interviewer, who has now become a producer, always seemed to be jinxed when it came to demonstration items. He was doing an interview with a representative of a firm making unbreakable glass and at the duly appointed time he walked up to this large sheet of plate glass and biffed it with a hammer. It shattered into a million pieces! Another time he was doing an item on burglar alarms. Could he make that alarm go off—no way! I was doing an interview on old railway posters and they were strung up all around my guest and myself. One fell, just at a crucial moment, narrowly missing my head. Animals nearly always let you down or steal the show. They seem to behave perfectly on rehearsal but by the time it gets to the real thing, either they're overcome by the heat (with all the lights studios are often very hot and uncomfortable) or just decide they've done their bit and invariably fall asleep. We had a gorgeous chimp on the programme one day. Delightful creature behaved perfectly and did everything he was supposed to do until we went on air and he did a bit more—defecated right in front of everyone!

Machines that have been working perfectly tend to give up the ghost when you're 'live'. The only thing to do is *ad-lib* your way out of it and pass on to another item. Despite its drawbacks I've always preferred 'live' television to recorded. With the latter you'll probably get a more polished end product but I love the immediacy of a live show and from what I can gather, so do the public.

Back to the Pebble Mill day. The programme went on air from 1.00 to 1.45 pm. Then we'd take the guests for a sandwich and a drink in the Editor's office. If you were engaged in interesting conversation past the time when you should have vacated the office, the cleaning lady would make her presence felt with the hoover. Then at 2.45 pm it was back into the office for a meeting about the next day's programme and that was when you'd discover what your particular item would be. If it were a book review you'd have the rest of that day to do your reading. A researcher would always have done a preliminary read and written out suggested questions but when it was a book item I preferred to be doubly sure and read the book myself. The meeting ended at 3.30 and then there would be 'fan' mail to attend to or a chat with the researcher about the next day's programme. We were usually free by around 4.30. Sometimes I'd go back to the flat and sleep for an hour or two, then eat something and have a look at the work for the next day. In two years in Birmingham, Marian and I went out less than half a dozen times. We were usually too tired, also when you've living between two homes it's not easy to establish a social life. I am quite convinced that the average worker in a 9 to 5 job has a better *social* life than most folk in broadcasting.

37

I've already said that I thoroughly enjoy interviewing authors and people from the world of entertainment. There was plenty of that on *Pebble Mill* and it was the part of the job that I enjoyed most. I met so many fascinating people—Robert Morley, Beryl Grey, Andy Williams, Hardy Kruger, Frank Finlay, Jim Dale, Louis Feraud the designer, William Rushton, Sacha Distel, Charles Aznavour, Sammy Cahn, Bud Freeman, Danny La Rue—as well as all the talented sculptors, painters and craftsmen it was my pleasure to interview.

I think the most memorable event for me was the day I met Omar Sharif, for years one of my favourite film stars. I had hoped very much that I would be given the interview but it was decided that Donny Macleod should do it. Donny commuted down to Birmingham from Aberdeen each week by 'plane. As fate would have it, on this particular day his 'plane was delayed. I was sitting at my desk waiting for my guest of the day to arrive, the actor Jim Dale, when the Assistant Editor. Jim Dumighan (now the Editor of the programme) approached me and asked if I would mind getting down to the studio and doing the chat with Omar. Mind! I fair flew those few steps to the lobby. I didn't even stop to go to make-up. I'd had no time to look at any research notes but happily had bought a copy of his book *The Eternal Male* a couple of months previously so I did have some background on him. He was actually in Birmingham to promote his backgammon sets for children at the Toy Fair at the National Exhibition Centre, so the interview was geared to that topic but I did manage to talk to him about his race-horses, his son, and his rather lonely life. I think the interview was a good one. I understand that he rang the next day to express his appreciation.

Again, please don't get the idea that it was all fun. Interviewing is difficult work. So many outside influences can affect it. So much can and does go wrong. I don't think I have ever, in fourteen years of broadcasting, been thoroughly satisfied with anything I've done and I've often gone home stewing over where things had gone wrong and cursing myself for not getting the best out of an interview. It's such a frustrating business because you always feel you could have done better and invariably the clock is against you. It takes time to establish a relationship with a guest and sometimes you're just getting into your stride when you see the floor manager giving you the wind up and that's that.

I remember one occasion on *Report West* when I did an unsatisfactory interview. It was on a Friday evening and I fretted and agonized over it the whole weekend. On the Monday morning I went straight into the Editor, Ron Evans, and apologized again for the Friday disaster. 'For Goodness sake, woman' he said, 'that went into the ether over forty-eight hours ago—FORGET IT'. And he's right you know. It's done and gone and the only thing is to try and see that similar mistakes don't occur again. I often think we, the people who make the programmes, worry far more about mistakes than the watching or listening public. In fact during the *Report West* days Bruce and I used to get the occasional letter of appreciation from our viewers expressing their enjoyment at the odd mistake. At least it showed we were, 'live' and human!

While at *Pebble Mill*, I was asked to do another series of *The Food Programme*. Fortunately for me, the *Pebble Mill* Editor agreed and I would catch the 'plane from Birmingham Airport to Glasgow on a Thursday night for a day's work on the Friday. During the second series I found myself involved in some single-subject programmes. What fun they were! One programme was about a small hotel in the Lake district near Ambleside called *Rothay Manor*. The owner, Bronwen Nixon, was a great character and she decided that during the leaner winter months she'd have 'special' weekends of gastronomic delight. One of these was to be 'Georgian', and it rather appealed to Mike the producer. We went up one weekend in November to do a reccé (that's sussing out the surroundings and the content so as to plan the most effective and economic filming plot). The next weekend we went back to make the film. We stayed at the hotel for the weekend, of course, as did some of the guests but others were locals who just came to partake of the magnificent food.

Rothay Manor is itself Georgian and lent itself to the occasion very well. Bronwen also liked her guests to dress the part even if it were a mere suggestion of the period. I was completely togged out in a lovely Georgian gown from the BBC's Wardrobe Department and of course I had a wig to cover my urchin cut.

The guests arrived around seven and were offered a glass of hot punch. I found it undrinkable. I don't like sweet drinks at all and apparently in the Georgian period, because sugar was so expensive and eminently sought after, the rich drowned everything in sugar to show their affluence. For authenticity, Bronwen's punch was extremely sweet. I think I was probably the only one who didn't enjoy it! The dining room looked magnificent. Tables groaned under silver plate and candelabra and I almost lost count of the different drinking glasses beside each plate.

The food was magnificent. The soup and fish course were followed by a refreshing lemon sorbet. There was a choice of venison or Captain Kidder's game pie for the main course complemented by the most tastily garnished vegetables and

39

potatoes. The sweet trolley was a tremendous sight offering a choice of six mouth-watering creations—all amazingly sweet. Then there was cheese, if you could possibly face any more food; followed by nuts and fruit. That came to seven courses and with almost every course there was a different wine, culminating in a dessert wine served from bottles with ice on the outside. Dessert wines would always be chilled and the ice gave a really dramatic effect. Somewhere along the line, I interviewed Bronwen at the dinner table; just in case you're wondering whether I did any work. Then we repaired to the lounge for coffee and musical entertainment in the Georgian mode. All the women were presented with heart-shaped candy boxes made from icing sugar and filled with home made petit fours. They were really a knock out.

The next morning's breakfast was so big it would have kept me going all day—eggs, bacon, sausage, black pudding, tomatoes, mushrooms, fried bread. I declined and delicately picked at some toast. At 10.30 there was a lecture on Georgian silver given by a local antique dealer and this was followed by coffee and Georgian style cakes. Even though we were busy filming, in the kitchens and elsewhere, there was still time to enjoy ourselves. I often think I've enjoyed life more, when I've been working on an interesting subject and with a great team, than I do when I'm off duty. The odd hours and constant necessity to move around can make a life in broadcasting a super one.

There was another splendid filming experience during *The Food Programme* and that took place on the beautiful West Coast of Scotland. I don't think it's generally known that the Scots fish some pretty exotic sea-food around their shores and, strangely, much of it is exported. One old fisherman told me that he remembered the days when they threw scampi back over the side!! They don't now though—a great deal of it is exported to the Mediterranean. Some of the fish they catch don't look particularly attractive and this often puts the housewife off buying it—although with world resources ever dwindling—I think visual barriers will have to be overcome. Anyway, they have a very rich seafood harvest up North and they celebrate by having a 'Seafood Festival'. Mike decided to film it. It was idyllic weather when he picked me up at Glasgow airport and drove me to Crinan where I hastily changed my clothes and presented myself on the roof balcony of the hotel to be filmed sampling a delicious dish called 'Scallops Henry Morgan'—scallops cooked in Champagne. And don't run away with the idea that we enjoyed *Cordon Bleu* cookery wherever we went for the food programme. The good food was the exception—the rule was a grabbed sandwich, curling at the edges, and an indifferent cup of coffee.

The day after the 'Scallops Henry Morgan', we drove over to the Galley of Lorne to film the Festival proper. That was a great day too with colourful local folk, a couple of glasses of Black Velvet (champagne and Guinness provided by a well-known firm!) not to mention the fish. Half way through the day the local Laird announced over the microphone that a bomb had decimated the pier at neighbouring Crinan. We all presumed it was some kind of joke until we returned to the hotel at Crinan in the evening. Sure enough, there was the pier in a sorry state, listing to one side. Apparently what happened was that a local fisherman had netted a barnacle-encrusted explosive device left over from the last war. The Navy had relieved him of it and detonated it at the end of the pier with cracking results! Some local wag is reported to have asked the commanding officer if his name was Mainwaring (from the character in *Dad's Army* who somehow always did things the wrong way with disastrous results).

It's very strange how work breeds work. If you're out of it, no-one seems to want to know, but if you're already sailing along quite happily working away then sure as eggs are eggs you'll be asked to do more. During the *Pebble Mill* period, my old chum from Bristol days, Brian Skilton, who was by now a television producer with the BBC in Plymouth, asked me to do a short series of programmes called *Zodiac and Co.* The idea of the programme was to have a panel of an astrologer, a graphologist and a palmist and a couple of mystery guests about whom the panel would be given the barest details and from which they would construct a brief analysis. The idea was to see how accurately they would assess the career, character, etc, of the guest. It was a kind of astrological *What's My Line?*. My job was to present the show, move it along and generally supply the glue. It was great fun to do and indeed, even as I write, I've just recorded four more. We've done twenty programmes spread over two years and have had characters such as John Cleese, Tim Brooke Taylor, Annabel Leventon, Fiona Richmond, Joan Bakewell, Wayne Sleep, the Bishop of Crediton and the Chief Constable of Devon and Cornwall. Although we only do four or five programmes in each short series, it's lovely to go back each time, meet the team and slip into the programme rather like donning a comfortable garment that's worn-in and good to wear again.

I enjoyed the work on *Pebble Mill* tremendously but I wasn't too happy with my yo-yo existence of living in a minute and grotty little flat during the week and only returning home at weekends. I told you before that I'm a home body and temperamentally unsuited to a gypsy existence—although I would happily leave my home to go *abroad* on a filming assignment. That's different. Unfortunately the Editor of the programme and I seemed to rub each other up the wrong way so the long and the short of it was that in 1978 I found myself out of work again, only this time it was worse than ever before. I had a mortgage to pay, no job, hadn't been well and was determined that I would only take a job back in Bristol or in London which is the Mecca of all broadcasting. I got some *cv's* printed (*curriculum vitae*—story of my working life) and settled down to the joyless task of writing letters to people in the business. I wrote about forty and received around twenty replies, all in the negative. 'That's it' I thought, 'I've had a good innings and this is the end of my broadcasting life'. But it wasn't. Late one night I received a 'phone call from the Presentation Editor of BBC Radio 1 and 2 asking me to meet him. The upshot was that Jimmy Kingsbury offered me a job as an announcer which meant reading news and doing continuity announcing. He gave me until the next day to make up my mind. As I was driving back to Chislehurst, where I was staying with an aunt, I heard Sheila Tracey reading the news on the radio. When I eventually reached home I rang her up and asked her about the job. We hadn't spoken to each other for almost ten years, since we were both down in Plymouth, but she was very helpful and told me what a great crowd of people they were on 1 and 2. That settled it and I accepted a year's contract the very next day. And Sheila was absolutely right about the people. I don't know whether it's because we work unsocial hours and there's a great *camaraderie* but I've never worked with a more friendly crowd. I thought that that would be the end of television work for me but indeed October 1978 to October 1979 was a most interesting year and I did much more than I anticipated. I was asked to present and interview on a BBC Midlands Current Affairs series which went out on a Friday night. This was one of my days off anyway and with Jimmy Kingsbury's permission, I was able to accept. Then I was asked to do the interviewing for the 1979 *Miss England* competition. That was hard work because the girls are usually very nervous and don't really like the interviewing part of the show. They don't get much time either—forty-five seconds to a minute is no time at all to establish a rapport and a girl's personality. However, I was also asked to do the *Miss United Kingdom* contest on which quite a few of the same girls appeared. I had much longer with them all and had time to build up their confidence. It meant working out questions for all the contestants although it would finally be only seven girls who'd appear for a television interview and I only knew which ones a couple of minutes before going on air. I enjoyed working on those programmes. It gave me an insight into the beauty game which I hadn't had before—a favourable one I might add. I saw no inkling of bitchiness, just a large number of pretty girls who wanted to win a competition—little different from any competition for a job except that they were selling their prettiness rather than their shorthand speeds or fluency in languages.

I was asked again to co-present the *Chelsea Flower Show* with Peter Seabrook for BBC2. On this occasion I really enjoyed myself. Having done the show the previous year, I was at least aware of the pitfalls and felt far more confident about it generally as well as having a better idea of the geography of the site—essential when you've got to present yourself at a given place in double quick time. I feel very privileged to have been able to see 'Chelsea' when it's not full of milling hordes of people. The show is breathtakingly beautiful and to be able to view the stands from a distance without interruption from a load of bobbing heads is something to be envied.

I thought I'd done everything open to me in broadcasting. I never imagined I'd end up as a DJ. However, Radio 2 launched itself into twenty-four hour broadcasting in 1979 and the three hours which had not been previously filled between 2.00 and 5.00 am were taken over by a programme called *You and the Night and the Music* and it was decided that seven of the Radio 2 announcers would each present one programme a week. I was asked in the April if I would do one. I'm no stranger to *ad-libbing* but I am to operating discs and tapes. However, through watching some of my colleagues and by spending several hours with a helpful Technical Operator in an empty Continuity Suite, I got the hang of the mechanics. I thoroughly enjoy doing the programme. There's an immediacy with radio which one loses in television because of all the technical paraphernalia. With *YATNAM'*, as we call it, there's just me, the microphone, the two technical gentlemen next door looking after tapes and making sure the balance is right, and the listener. It's difficult to ascertain the number of our audience because if they're shift workers listening to *'YATNAM'* they're unlikely to be around at the time of day when audience research people do their work. All I can say is that our audience may be small but is a very appreciative and devoted one and it's a good feeling to think that you may be brightening up the wee small hours for people unable to sleep, people in pain, lonely people or those who simply work odd hours.

I'm sure I speak for most of my colleagues, behind and in front of the camera or microphone, when I say that apart from the obvious desire to build up a career and earn a living in an interesting medium there is also a great satisfaction in feeling that you are doing something for people even if it's only entertaining or enlightening them for a few seconds.

And, in this business, you never know what's around the corner. At the beginning of this year I was invited to read the national News on BBC Television, on a four-month attachment from Radio.

What superb experience it was, working with such a dedicated and expert team, under considerable pressure most of the time. And I felt privileged to be involved in reporting some of the stories which will make the history books of the future.

Conclusion

'So what's it all about Alfie?' I can't really answer that. All I know is that broadcasting in general is like a drug. On so many occasions when I've been out of work I've thought of getting out of the business but I always end up 'hooked' again.

I haven't achieved as much as I would like and I don't know what the future holds. As a freelance, I have no security of job nor a pension to look forward to, other than one I might provide for myself if ever I could save enough money to afford the premiums! What I do know is that I count myself extremely fortunate to have had as many years as I have working in a medium that I love, and find stimulating and exciting. I have interviewed some wonderful people, I've worked with so many 'characters', been privy to a 'peep behind the scenes' on many stories and obtained an insight into so many things which otherwise would have passed me by. I've been chilled to the marrow while out filming, roasted to a turn in excruciatingly hot studios and had sleepless nights before certain interviews. I've cried with frustration at times, I've been worried sick over where the next job and pay cheque would come from but I've laughed a great deal too and I've *never ever* been *bored*.

A career in broadcasting

Well, you're obviously asking yourself 'How do I get into broadcasting?' That's the million dollar question and of course will depend on just what you think you ultimately want to do. Although being 'on screen' or behind a microphone might seem to be the ultimate goal for many young folk, I can assure you that, if I had my time again I would opt for the production side which is in many ways more creative. After all the Editor or producer is the one who makes the decisions and creates the programmes. Don't forget that for every broadcaster there are dozens of 'behind the scenes' folk, all performing valuable and interesting tasks.

Basic requirements for a television programme would include design; graphics; scenery (in studio); lighting; cameras; recording and editing facilities; make-up; not to mention the administrative team of researchers, secretaries and producers. A Drama production has many more requirements on top of the basics; someone must attend to the casting, scripts, outside filming sequences, and continuity (for when a set is struck and has to be re-assembled later in exactly the same order). The lists of folk required are endless. In fact, the BBC Staff List of the principal Engineering, Production and Management staff in Television and Radio, both network and regional, and other departments includes only about a sixth of the total staff but still covers over eighty pages. Does that give you an idea of the vastness of the operation? Obviously, if you want to go into the engineering side, there are definite guidelines as to the academic qualifications required. With regard to other sides of the broadcasting business, there are *not many hard and fast rules*. Because there are none, I decided that the only way I could hope to give you a guideline would be by asking a representative cross section of people within television some basic questions. Obviously many of these folk are friends or work companions, some I approached because of the positions they have attained, and I thank them all warmly for sparing the time to fill in my questionnaire.

Programme Controller

Designation	PROGRAMME CONTROLLER, GRANADA TV
Name	*Mike Scott*
Qualifications	*Confined to good results in General School Certificate*

Mike did two years of National Service, six months with Unilever and then worked for a year as a stagehand/film extra while trying to get a Union ticket in order to become a trainee film editor. He finally did get into television as a production trainee (sweeping floors, tracking cameras, working booms, etc). From there he moved on for a short period as a cameraman. Afterwards he worked as floor manager; director; presenter (you might even remember him on *Cinema*, among other programmes); producer/performer; exective producer; executive producer/reporter (*Nuts and Bolts of the Economy*); deputy programme controller; and finally programme controller. All this has taken Mike twenty-four years to achieve—and what an achievement!

Job satisfaction

Constantly changing problems. The stimulation of being involved with 'hopefully' new ideas. The mixed pleasure of picking yourself up, brushing yourself down and ·starting all over again after something which hasn't worked. Barring periods of stagnation, the consolation of working in an expanding and successful industry, is most satisfying.

Advice

The whole 'trick' is learning to get through 'boards' (interviews). This is an acquired skill which involves having something exciting to talk about in terms of past experience. The technique is that your interviewers will forget the questions they were going to ask you if you stimulate them enough with your own past. I'm entirely serious about this. It means that you are unlikely to succeed before you are 21 or even older. The years between education and applying to get into television should be spent in work experience which will broaden your horizons and give you a chance to observe and talk about things in which other people will be interested.

Designation	PROGRAMME CONTROLLER, HTV WEST
Name	*Ron Evans*
Qualifications	*Less than nil*

Ron Evans was my boss for six years and although he proclaims that his qualifications are 'less than nil', I know him to be an extremely intelligent, intuitive and gifted man.

Ron's background is journalistic. He worked both in the provinces and Fleet Street on weekly, morning, evening and Sunday papers—experience that was totally relevant and necessary to his work in television. He's worked as a programme researcher and editor. I worked for him when he was head of News and Current Affairs and in the three years since I left HTV West, he became head of Regional Programmes and is now programme controller.

Job satisfaction

Ron says that I would need another book to detail all his job satisfaction! He finally reduced his comments to 'Essentially the exercise of the privilege and responsibility of being the middle man, the "passer-on", between the news event, the happening, the entertainment, the drama, the whatever!—and the millions of viewers.'

Advice

Learn the basics well—whether in engineering, journalism, make-up etc, and then select your target. Follow it up with enthusiasm, hard work, and the resilience to overcome the knocks and disappointments. Never forget the viewer and *enjoy it.*

Editor, Television News

Designation   EDITOR, BBC TELEVISION NEWS
Name   *Alan H. Protheroe*
Qualifications   *Member of the British Institute of Management*

Alan worked as a newspaper reporter and sub-editor, freelance writer and soldier before entering television and feels that this was all relevant experience. He started work in 1957 and became editor, BBC TV News in 1977. During his years in television, Alan has worked as a reporter; newsreader; industrial correspondent; programme editor and scriptwriter, as well as in film and studio production. He declares that only 'God knows' what is his ultimate goal professionally.

Job satisfaction

'Unremitting work of a demanding intellectual nature; the utter unpredictability of every minute of the day. The sheer thrill of beating the hell out of the competition, and the enormous satisfaction of seeing what your team achieves, on the air, five times every day of every year.'

Advice

'If you want a quiet life; if you want to work regular hours; if you want to be able to plan your life ahead; if you don't have the courage to overcome personal danger and difficulty, *don't*, please, please, don't come into television or radio journalism. It simply is not for you. Start on a weekly newspaper: graduate to daily journalism. Learn what life is about. Be curious. Be thrilled by life and people...and maybe, maybe we'll have you...!'

Designation   HEAD OF LIGHT ENTERTAINMENT, GRANADA TV
Name   *John Hamp*
Qualifications   *First Class Diploma in Engineering*

John Hamp had a varied career doing publicity for Pathé Pictures, performing in a variety act, and working as a theatre manager and theatre producer before entering television. He feels that all this work was relevant experience and contributed towards his start in television as a producer. He later became an executive producer and it has taken him fifteen years to reach the position he now holds as head of Light Entertainment.

Job satisfaction

Working with artists and musicians is fun. High ratings and (good!) press notices contribute a great deal of satisfaction. John also likes to negotiate good deals and enjoys creative and artistic achievement.

Advice

You must really *want* to be in the business, otherwise it can be *hard* and sometimes *boring*. Be prepared to take some knocks. Be specific about what branch of the industry you want to enter—and study hard anything that is relevant to that subject. Study other people's work.

Music Director

Designation   MUSIC DIRECTOR, HTV WEST
Name   *Sydney Sager*
Qualifications   *ARCM*

Sydney Sager spent fifteen years playing in an army band, followed by a period as a trombonist at the Royal Opera House, Covent Garden. He has also worked as a freelance playing jazz, circuses, theatre, symphony orchestras and several years in a BBC Orchestra. Composing and conducting many scores for television dramas and documentary films have also come within his working spectrum. All his previous experience was obviously relevant to the position he now holds although he tells me it was not a position he sought but rather one that was offered to him. Now his goal is to develop the scope of music within television and he declares that he has a long way to go so he obviously wouldn't consider leaving the industry yet, although, he says, he could foresee a time when he might want to be free of the administrative aspects of working as a music director. He would, however, always wish to continue composing and conducting for television.

Job satisfaction

For Sydney, it lies in hearing the results of his work. 'When you know that what you have done is good, it is most rewarding to realise that it is there for the pleasure of an enormous audience. On the other hand, when you feel that you might have produced better music, the television recording is there to embarrass for as long as it's shown!'

Advice

Music in television covers a dauntingly wide area so you must maintain a lively and perceptive interest in *every* kind of music—nothing should be too way-out or popular or even banal for your attention—at the same time all facets of classical music should be known to you. Cultivate your own special fields but keep your mind and ear open to all that is going on in music. Experience in dealing with people of every kind is also helpful.

Designation   EDITOR, CURRENT AFFAIRS, HTV WEST
Name   *Bruce Hockin*
Qualifications   *Training as a journalist*

Bruce worked in weekly and daily newspapers and found this particularly relevant to his work in television first as a researcher/scriptwriter, then as a reporter/interviewer and then as a presenter of News and Current Affairs programmes where I met him and worked as his co-presenter on *Report West* for six years. Now I would have to show him deference as the editor of Current Affairs for HTV!

Job satisfaction

He's happy to be working in the business in which he always wanted to be involved. 'Every day is a New Day—aren't I a lucky fellow to be paid a handsome salary for something I enjoy so much?'!

Advice

Start at the bottom, learn and aim for the top! Never be afraid to ask for help and advice. Remember, a little humility goes a long way!

Assistant Editor

Designation	ASSISTANT EDITOR, PEBBLE MILL AT ONE, BBC TV
Name	*Peter Hercombe*
Qualifications	*Ten O levels;*
	Three A levels; Diploma of the National Council for the Training of Journalists

Peter worked with various National and provincial newspapers for six years and feels that the journalistic assessment of information and knowledge and how to process it in media terms was relevant to the work he did and does in television. It's taken him ten years to reach his present position and during that time he has worked variously as a Television News reporter, radio and Television News sub, Television News editor, Television producer and film director. He's not sure what is his ultimate goal although he feels he hasn't yet reached it. When asked if he would leave the industry, his answer was an emphatic *'no'*.

Job satisfaction

Lies in creative construction of storylines into a visually attractive programme/film; the excitement of mixing pictures and music together to create an emotional experience for the viewer; and knowing that your visual skills can create a simultaneous stimulation among millions of people. You can also present the viewer with information about which he was hitherto totally ignorant, eg journalistic, John Pilger's film on *Cambodia* at the time of that country's appalling tragedy in 1979.

Advice

Programme or film making experience cannot be rushed. Too many people, straight from film school or college believe they enter the industry as 'gifts from the Gods'. But it is a slow process of gradual maturing, and it may be many years before they're given free reign and allowed to go ahead on their own. The intervening years can be exceedingly frustrating, and a great deal of patience and perseverance is required.

Designation	PRODUCER, GENERAL FEATURES, BBC PLYMOUTH
Name	*Brian Skilton*
Qualifications	*Five O levels, One A level*
	One year at art school

Brian started out in radio and to use his own words 'worked my way up'. He began as a studio manager—playing records, doing the sound effects for drama, light entertainment and adjusting the output of microphones mainly for pop music. After five years he became a talks and features producer and during that time I did work for him on a morning programme in Bristol. He stayed in radio for another five years and then became a production assistant (director) and then a producer in television. Although Brian thoroughly enjoys his job he says that one day he might just take up painting again.

Job satisfaction

Although called a television producer, I choose also to direct most of the films that I produce. The work is essentially creative and the main satisfaction comes from seeing an idea change into a television programme. Through my work I'm continually meeting interesting people, many of them famous, and this is a constant pleasure and always stimulating. Television demands a high degree of team work and it is most rewarding to be one of a good team, all working for the same end. Equally, of course, it is most frustrating when someone lets the side down.

Advice

Television is very competitive, so it isn't going to be easy, especially if you hope to work on the production side. A good degree is not essential, but it makes it much easier to get started. If, like me, you are not originally well qualified, you will almost certainly have to start at the bottom and work your way up. However, television is always hungry for talent, so if you really have talent, then you can make it, and the journey up should be great fun.

Amusing incidents

There tends to be a great deal of humour around when people are under the kind of pressure involved in filming and studio work.

Because of the high standard of skills, things don't go wrong very often, and when they do, it's not always funny. However, I remember filming with Tony Soper who was standing on top of a Dartmoor bog explaining how the whole thing was floating, and that if the surface broke you'd fall in but could escape with a swimming motion. I told camera and sound to keep running if Tony did sink into the bog, but although he was rocking the whole surface, it didn't give way. When he had finished, the sound recordist who was always most particular, decided he needed to get closer to record the splashing as Tony rocked about. With the camera turned off I would have been most unhappy if Tony had ended up wet and muddy when we still had a good deal of filming to do. As I turned to the sound recordist to see if he was happy with his recording, the bog gave way. Tony remained safely on a tussock of grass as the sound man sank gracefully into three foot of slime!! All in a day's work!

Designation	SENIOR PRODUCER, BBC TV
Name	*Jill Roach*
Qualifications	*BA (Hons)*

After leaving university Jill did some teaching which she says was no help at all when she was trying to get into television. She succeeded, however, and over a ten year period went through the stages of being a researcher and a production assistant (director) before becoming a producer. At the time of writing, Jill is the producer in charge of the children's news programme *John Craven's Newsround*.

Job satisfaction

One hundred per cent. 'There can't be many more interesting things to do than to see a programme grow from nothing to a real, living, hopefully successful, programme.'

Advice

Try and find out enough about television so that you can decide what area interests you most. Then, keep writing and 'pestering' (her own word) people until you get in. Write direct to producers if necessary as personnel people may not always be able to help. Also, don't forget the need for a union card in ITV!

Producer, Further Education

Designation PRODUCER, FURTHER EDUCATION, BBC TV
Name *Jenny Rogers*
Qualifications *BA, DPSA*

Jenny was a teacher before entering the world of television and feels that this experience was relevant to her present work because as she says 'It's all communication'. She was education officer for the BBC and now produces programmes for the Further Education Department.

Job satisfaction

Lies in never doing the same thing from one day to the next; in learning new things all the time; working in a medium and for an organisation that enjoys high public esteem; and 'Considerable freedom to be my own boss'!

Advice

Make sure you are the sort of person who really can work in a team and can communicate clearly and easily to others. Have a realistic idea of what the work involves and be self critical but confident.

Designation PRODUCER, GENERAL FEATURES, BBC TV
Name *Patricia Houlihan*
Qualifications *Ten O and two A levels from St Joseph's Convent Grammar School... but not much else*

On leaving school Patricia worked in minor capacities for *The Times*, *The Observer*, and on publicity for a publishing group. She says that although this was not part of a 'master-plan', it turned out to be extremely relevant—more by luck than judgement. She's now done all types of research, production and film direction over ten years in television (hard labour she calls it!). Her goal was to become a BBC television producer—she's done it and she wouldn't consider leaving the industry.

Job satisfaction

This is seeing something you've tried to achieve turning out not only as you'd hoped, but a great deal better.

Patricia has worked, among other things, on the Parkinson programme and on some of Esther Rantzen's *The Big Time*.

Advice

She sees quite a number of youngsters who wish to enter television and her advice is always to 'think again' because the medium has been glamourised. 'However, there are rewards, it just takes much longer than you'd think to reach the stage where you're in line for some of them, (unless you're incredibly lucky)'.

Designation	PRODUCER — OUTSIDE BROADCASTS, BBC TV
Name	*Michael Lumley*
Qualifications	*Degree in Mathematics*

Michael worked as a school teacher and feels that this work was helpful to him when he joined the BBC as a production assistant in Educational Broadcasting. His next step was to become an assistant producer — all in all it took him seven years to reach the rank of producer with Outside Broadcasts. At the time of writing Michael is doing work covering royal occasions and big outside functions like *The Chelsea Flower Show*. (And having worked on the latter I realize just how much organization has to go into a venture of that kind — it's a mammoth task!)

Job satisfaction

Michael's own word was 'vanity' — seeing a project through from start to finish — plus all the obvious bonuses of doing a creative job.

Advice

Be persistent. If you can't get the job you want — try one at a lower level of responsibility — it's much easier (but can still be *very* difficult) to progress from within the BBC.

Designation	RESEARCH ASSISTANT, PEBBLE MILL AT ONE
	BBC TV
Name	*Clare Stride*
Qualifications	*Three days at Art School*
	Eighteen months at University

Clare has been in the BBC for three years. She started as a secretary in Radio Documentaries Department and then progressed to *Pebble Mill*, again in a secretarial capacity. Once working on the programme she moved into the position of producer's assistant and from there has become a Researcher. She would like to produce or do film direction and because of the BBC's excellent 'attachment' scheme, she is going on a film course which will of course help her, in the future, to achieve her ambition.

Job satisfaction

The variety of items you can research—art, science, and different 'personalities'. You meet different people and travel to cities which you would otherwise not have visited. Another element which appeals to Clare is the quickness with which the situation can change so that boredom never has a chance to set in.

Advice

To have as varied interests as possible; the ability to adapt; and the interest in working with different people. It is necessary to have a good education, although Clare doesn't think that a degree is essential. One must have enthusisam and the ability to write well. Clare says that working in a factory, garage and shops for however short a time helped her to have a wider view of life than if she'd gone into the BBC straight from cloistered university life.

Amusing incidents

(Clare was in charge of the *Pebble Mill* farm at the back of the studios.) 'I had forgotten to clip the wings of the guinea fowl to prevent them flying away from the cameras. Two minutes before we were to record the item, I heard this enormous flutter of wings, looked round, and the whole lot were up in the trees!

'Another time I put in a request for a Jersey cow and got what looked like a bullock which promptly took off, with the interviewee in tow. There was never a dull moment!'

Research Assistant

Designation	RESEARCH ASSISTANT, PEBBLE MILL AT ONE BBC TV
Name	*Stephen Weddle*
Qualifications	*BSc Sociology*

Steve did research into Sociology of Medicine at Bedford College, University of London; worked as an education welfare officer for ILEA in Kentish Town, North London, and also took a job as a reporter on the *Birmingham Post and Mail*. He says that the journalistic experience at the *Post* provided good grounding in searching out items for *Pebble Mill*. He also worked as a radio journalist on BBC Radio Stoke-on-Trent before joining the *Pebble Mill* team as a research assistant in 1976. (I'd like to add that Steve is one of the most thorough researchers I've worked with.)

He says his goal is to be a producer and that he'd only consider leaving the industry on 'bad days'!

Job satisfaction

Consistent variety of work on a magazine programme. 'An example was a recent week when I was involved with a marching girls band one day and the next doing an item on Einstein'. There are occasions when items can influence or move viewers to a new awareness of important issues. Examples include an early item on the Northern Ireland Peace People with Betty Williams and the first Network look at the work of the anti-whaling campaigners, 'Greenpeace'. There's also a great deal of satisfaction in meeting the many fascinating people who come to appear on *Pebble Mill at One*. (Hear, hear—I second that!)

Advice

Don't give up! Competition to get into television is very intense and it requires some persistence and even 'bloody-mindedness' to break down the doors. Don't take 'No' for an answer. Make yourself such a nuisance that they have to say 'yes'.

Amusing incidents

These are only amusing in retrospect—at the time of happening they're horrific! Like the Japanese who came to show his exotic fish but spoke about as much English as the fish he loved. Every question was greeted with an inscrutable oriental grin. Then there

60

was the mad inventor who demonstrated his egg-cracking device, depositing the yolk into a tin of smoker's toothpaste, which was to come next in the item to demonstrate a smoker's toothpaste dispenser!

Principal Production Assistant

Designation   PRINCIPAL PRODUCTION ASSISTANT
                   YORKSHIRE TV
Name   *Doreen Killon*
Qualifications *Two O levels*
                   One A level

Doreen started work at the age of 15 as a clerk/typist. She went to evening classes to get her O and A levels and also her shorthand. Then she says she worked in various boring commercial firms, first as a shorthand typist, then as a secretary. She went to France out of sheer boredom and worked as an au pair for a while returning to England determined to get a more interesting job. She drove the newspaper (NATSOPA) union agency insane by turning up every day asking for temporary or permanent employment. Finally she got a temp-sec job at the *Daily Express* where they eventually asked her to stay, as secretary to their Woman's Page Editor. Doreen remained with the Express Group for eight years doing many interesting jobs ending up as secretary to the foreign editor of the Sunday Express. Boredom set in again and she decided to try television. She got a short-lived job as secretary to the head of Drama at Rediffusion—short-lived because four months later they lost their franchise. Her boss asked her to join him in setting up the Drama Department at Yorkshire Television. After eighteen months she was asked to apply to be trained as a PA. Doreen feels that all the jobs she's done, including the boring ones, have helped her to appreciate how marvellous it is to enjoy and look forward to her work. She says that no other job in television would interest her more than the one she's doing and adds, modestly, that even after ten years she's still learning.

Job satisfaction

PAs at YTV work on *all* programmes so Doreen works on everything from Sport and Education to Live News, big Light Entertainment and one-off dramas. She says that the more experience you get the more you can 'help' and 'add' to the content of a programme and its presentation and she gets a great kick out of knowing that an idea she put forward actually worked and improved the programme. Satisfaction also comes from the immense variety of work and the people she meets.

Advice

Never give up trying to get in. Determination *does* work in the end. Take *any* job offered to you no matter how menial. It's then up to you to prove it's worth the company's while to try you out in something better. Choose a hobby which will help you within television— work in an amateur dramatic group. Spend some of your spare time watching the work of whichever department you'd like to join, eg as secretary to the Head of Drama and even as a trainee PA Doreen spent every evening and some weekends sitting-in on other Production Assistants' programmes. An encouraging example is a young boy who used to be in the post room at YTV who spent every spare moment watching the film editors at work. Now he's an assistant film editor!

Amusing incidents

'After ten days' training as a PA, in the news section, I thought I'd never learn and I'd made a terrible mistake so I resigned! (My resignation wasn't accepted.)'

Producer's Assistant

Designation PRODUCER'S ASSISTANT, BBC TV
Name Eleanor Taylor
Qualifications *Four O levels, one Higher, Scottish National Diploma in Business Studies*

Eleanor joined the BBC straight from school as a secretary and it has taken her four years to become a producer's assistant. She says that 'it would have to be a tremendous job to pull her away from working in television', but she's not sure about an ultimate goal.

Job satisfaction

Teamwork. Meeting different types of people; seeing the end product; and the feeling of involvement one gets.

Advice

Be keen to learn and be willing. You must have the ability to get along with others and be able to compromise. It's helpful if you have an outgoing personality and you must be adaptable.

Designation	SENIOR MAKE-UP ARTIST, BBC TV BIRMINGHAM
Name	*Gwen Arthy*
Qualifications	*Six years art school—took no exams*

Gwen is in charge of the make-up Department in Birmingham, which, as a Network Production Centre, has a high Light Entertainment and Drama output, so make-up work is varied. She was in theatre stage management making headdresses, false noses, plaster casts and scene painting before entering television.

Job satisfaction

When asked about job satisfaction which is enormous because of the variety in the work, Gwen said 'And what about the frustrations? One always feels, if you could have another go, you could do better'.

Advice

You must be strong and healthy because conditions are hard— outside in all weather, then inside in hot stuffy studios. Hours are long and there's no such thing as weekends or bank holidays when you work a shift system. The BBC doesn't insist on As and Os but consideration is given to art students and beauticians and they must have a flair for theatre. Personality is important and the ability to deal with artistic temperament for the make-up room is one area where an actor, for instance, will want to relax or 'blow off steam'. Gwen suggests getting hold of an excellent book by Herman Buchman called *Film and TV Make-up*, published by Watson Guptill and marketed in this country by Pitman.

Senior Make-up Artist (freelance)

Designation SENIOR MAKE-UP ARTIST (FREELANCE)
Name *Valerie Elliott*
Qualifications *Four O levels*
Five RSA exams

Val has had quite a varied work background. Her first job was as a demonstrator for a perm and colour manufacturer. She trained to be a make-up artist with the BBC and then moved out of that field into working as an assistant and then a fully fledged floor manager. She then left broadcasting for a spell to work as an air hostess. She returned to make-up and got a job with HTV West in Bristol where she worked for several years before leaving to join Yorkshire Television as a senior make-up artist.

Job satisfaction

Helping artists relax before a programme (she certainly did plenty of that for me when I was at HTV)—giving them confidence etc. Val enjoys anything challenging in the make-up line particularly character make-ups and period hairstyles.

Advice

Try and obtain the necessary O and A levels and do a two year course in hairdressing and beauty culture at Technical College. Armed with these qualifications see if you can gain a place on a BBC Make-up Training Scheme.

Amusing incidents

'While working in Glasgow for the BBC, I was making up extras for a period drama. One old man sat in my make-up chair—I was just about to fit him with a wig when he said 'Oh, excuse me please', and promptly popped his glass eye into the palm of his hand! *Quelle horreur!*'

Designation   SCENIC DESIGNER, BBC TV
Name   *Roger Murray-Leach*
Qualifications   *Trained as architect to Intermediate Level*

Roger worked for two and a half years as an architectural assistant and got a good grounding in architectural styles; structure; and a training to observe, which served him well for television. He spent four years as an assistant and has now been a designer with the BBC for ten years.

Job satisfaction

Satisfaction comes from covering a vast spectrum of design and an ability to reflect personalities of characters hugely different from one's own. He has increased his knowledge, through research for programmes, in areas that he otherwise would not have touched. And of course there's the satisfaction of designing a product that is seen by a very large public.

Advice

An aspiring designer needs art, architectural, interior design or theatre training. The time taken to rise from assistant to designer has increased over the last few years so a person intending to become a designer must be '*prepared to wait*'.

Graphic Artist

Designation	GRAPHIC ARTIST (FREELANCE)
Name	*Andrea Cooper*
Qualifications	*Five O levels*
	Two A levels
	LSIA

Andrea did various jobs in advertising and photography before entering the field of television in which she's now worked for four years.

Job satisfaction

Variety! Working in a creative environment with a large proportion of extrovert people is most satisfying. You gain experience very rapidly because you're always working against the clock.

Advice

Fifty per cent of the job is getting on with people. Be adaptable! If it's at all possible try and get to know someone in the business before you start because they can explain some of the 'wrinkles'.

Always be prepared to learn (know-alls are no good!). Work hard.

Designation   LIGHTING DIRECTOR, YORKSHIRE TV
Name   *John M. Watt*
Qualifications *City and Guilds Final in Mechanical Engineering*

John worked in mechanical engineering and theatre stage management and lighting. He says that the theatre work was relevant experience when he joined television. He worked for five years as a technical trainee; engineering assistant and trainee lighting director before becoming a junior lighting director. All in all he's worked in the industry for fifteen years and his goal is to be involved with the lighting of TV productions of a standard comparable with good movies. 'The industry hasn't got there yet, so neither have I' says John.

Job satisfaction

Total artistic picture, making satisfaction on a par with any of the arts and crafts. The tremendous variety of people you meet and work with on both sides of the camera—articulate, intelligent and fun. Also there's a similar variety in the types of programme on which you work. Mixed hours (wrongly called unsocial!).

Advice

Be aware that you will probably always be an 'employee' because there aren't many ways of 'starting up on your own'. Learn about all the subjects involved on the fringes of your central interest. A lighting man needs a knowledge of sound; electronics; engineering; music; photography; design; scenic construction; staff management, etc, etc. Get into a television company in a junior position (after obtaining as many qualifications as you are able) and *observe*.

Technical Manager/Lighting Director

Designation   TECHNICAL MANAGER/LIGHTING DIRECTOR
BBC TV
Name   *Errol Patrick Ryan*
Qualifications   *City and Guilds Full Technological Certificate in Telecommunications*

Errol worked in telecommunications and telegraphy before entering television and in the twelve years since he joined the BBC he has worked as a studio engineer; telecine operator; vision operator; lighting console operator; vision supervisor and technical manager. His ultimate goal is to be a lighting director on plays of the highest complexity. He realises this will take at least another six or seven years to achieve and declares that he wouldn't leave the television industry 'even for money'!

Job satisfaction

Working in television is interesting and very satisfying. What must be remembered about all operational jobs in television is that an error can instantly be seen by millions of viewers. This is a sobering thought and certainly puts pressure on the individual to get his contribution to the programme right. The satisfaction comes from helping in the making of a programme people like or you hope that they will like.

I can recall those early rocket launches to the moon and seeing the huge rocket standing on it's launching pad, and listening to the countdown '10, 9, 8…and then 4, 3, 2, 1, Liftoff'. Who, watching, wasn't full of expectancy and excitement…will it or won't it shoot into the air? Well, in fact the countdown process happens every day in television studios; flashing red lights, and in the case of 'live' programmes, watching for the cue dots that tell you when your programme is going on the air. The whole team is concentrated and excited…4, 3, 2, 1, *cut*, 'We're on the air, Studio.' It's all fairly sick-making when it goes wrong, but very satisfying when it's right.

Advice

Try and organize a visit to the television studios near your home. Decide what technical area you'd like to work in. Find out what qualifications are needed and concentrate hard on passing the appropriate exams.

Remember that supply and demand are key words for any group in TV. Try and find out where there is most need. If it is not quite the job you want, remember that once within the industry it is easier to cross over to another affiliated technical area.

70

Designation   TECHNICAL MANAGER, BBC TV BIRMINGHAM
Name   *Derek Price*
Qualifications   *Five O levels and three A levels*
                    City and Guilds Telecommunications Certificate

Derek worked as a radar technician in the RAF which he says was vaguely relevant experience when he came to join the BBC. Over a period of seventeen years, he has done every job in technical operations, ie cameraman, sound supervisor, vision supervisor, and videotape editor.

Job satisfaction

There's a great deal of job satisfaction, both artistically—painting with light can be very rewarding—and technically—in the organization of planning and getting a big show off the ground.

Advice

Think about the life style. If you like a regular, well-ordered life, with regular hours then this is not for you. If you can accept working very irregular hours, nights and weekends then 'Yes'. Don't have a fixed idea of what you want to do—the opportunities are unlimited.

Amusing incidents

At the Hippodrome Circus, Yarmouth, in a hurry to change a monitor, running, from a brightly lit circus ring to the dark artists' entrance, straight into an elephant's behind!

     At a classical concert, a large camera dolly was being driven by a relatively inexperienced operator. It was getting closer and closer to the harp. The harpist remained in focus until the very last moment when the camera went straight through the harp. (Not funny for the harpist!)

Film Lighting Cameraman

Designation   FILM LIGHTING CAMERAMAN, YORKSHIRE TV
Name   *Frank Alan Pocklington*
Qualifications   *None*

Between 1947-57 Alan worked as a photo journalist on a magazine called *Picture Post* which he felt was relevant experience for his next job as he considered film in television to be the natural progression from photojournalism when *Picture Post* ceased publication. For a time he worked as a freelance lighting cameraman for the BBC *Tonight* programme. He's been in his present position for eleven years as a film lighting cameraman on documentaries and drama productions for Yorkshire Television. Alan has a goal which is to see the film cameraman in television receive true credit for his enormous contribution, particularly in documentaries.

Job satisfaction

It is a truly creative job which many people would consider glamorous. There's a great deal of travelling, total involvement and it's stimulating.

Advice

Television is an industry with a wide cross-section of talented folk drawn from newspapers, live theatre, feature film industry and electronic engineering fields and this mix can, at times, produce conflicting ideas. If you don't have qualifications of a trade which would fit into any of these areas, well then you could always start in the post and messengers department and look around. Be warned—the competition is very stiff.

Amusing incidents

I had gone on a brief fishing trip in a tribal canoe (filming of course) when a Carib Indian Chief took a fancy to my boots which I'd left on a rock above the water line. On returning to the shore, I found a colleague haggling over a price for the boots—he always had an eye for the main chance! I managed to convince the chief that my friend was affected by the sun and we parted company with the boots safely on my own feet.

Designation CAMERAMAN, BBC TV
Name *Norman Steemson*
Qualifications *Seven O levels*
Two A levels
City and Guilds Photography Diploma

Norman worked in electronics and photography before entering the world of television as an assistant cameraman. He worked as such for three years before becoming a cameraman in which capacity he's now worked for four years. And his goal is to do television lighting or production.

Job satisfaction

It's creative and there's a wide variety of work. You come into contact with interesting people and there's a high level of personal responsibility.

Advice

Take a keen interest in photography; hi-fi; electronics; the cinema and theatre.

Designation	HEAD OF SOUND, HTV WEST
Name	*Michael Gore*
Qualifications	*City and Guilds Telecommunications*

Michael worked for Imhofs in television and radio servicing. He also did a period of service with the Royal Air Force and during that time started a Forces Radio Network at RAF Horsham St Faith which of course was helpful to him when he entered the world of television in 1957. He started as a sound trainee with ATV and worked up through the grades. He was sound supervisor with an Outside Broadcast unit for several years and was responsible for sound coverage of the Investiture of the Prince of Wales.

HTV West are very strong on the documentary and drama making scene so Michael would be in charge of organizing sound for the big events both in studio and 'on the road'.

Job satisfaction

Lies in working with a large orchestra and professional artists. He also enjoys 'live' programmes and working with good directors.

Advice

Michael says this is difficult to answer but suggests that an aspirant should apply to the BBC as the best training ground. (Praise indeed for a man trained and raised in Independent Television.) He adds that to be a sound engineer one must have a good musical ear and be able to interpret arrangers' and musicians' ideas, as well as being a good technican.

Designation   SENIOR SOUND SUPERVISOR, BBC TV BIRMINGHAM
Name   *David Weir*
Qualifications   *Nine O levels*
One A level

David has worked in broadcasting for ten years. He started as a technical operator and progressed to studio manager, then on to audio assistant and audio supervisor. He's now working as a senior sound supervisor and hopes eventually to make the grade as light entertainment producer for television.

Job satisfaction

The job is both creative and artistic—and therefore rewarding. There's a constant challenge, especially in a place like *Pebble Mill* (BBC Birmingham studios) where producers are for ever trying to think up new and sometimes bizarre ideas. There is absolutely no routine and I've never had two days the same so it is very rarely boring. Obviously you get to work with interesting and famous people—the work is often exciting—but most of all it's *fun*.

Advice

1   A qualification in maths and physics will help.
2   Be prepared to start at the bottom and work up—often a slow process!
3   For anyone really interested, make a phone call to an audio manager or personnel officer and try to arrange a guided tour. Also try to meet and speak with people who are actually doing the job.

Stage Manager/Floor Manager, Outside Broadcasts

Designation   OUTSIDE BROADCASTS STAGE MANAGER
        FLOOR MANAGER, BBC TV BIRMINGHAM
        BIRMINGHAM
Name   *Steve Pierson*
Qualifications *Five O levels*

Steve went straight from school into television as a floor assistant. Then he became a trainee assistant/floor manager and later worked in the studio operations section of scenic services group to gain experience of construction and handling of scenery and props. He's been in the industry for fifteen years and has latterly been on training attachments as an Outside Broadcasts stage manager. He says he would like to direct but that he would miss the variety and satisfaction gained from his present responsibilities.

Job satisfaction

Steve enjoys the irregular hours of work and the variety of programmes—motor racing; rowing; *Match of the Day*; golf; general elections; *Pebble Mill*; *Saturday Night at the Mill*; *Young Scientist of the Year*; and *Pot Black*—just to mention a few. Every day is different with new problems to be overcome—every day is a challenge with a sense of achievement when the transmission light goes out after a hard but interesting day.

Advice

Join for the right reasons! Television may sound like a 'glamorous' career but it can be very demanding. Evidence of interest in broadcasting eg being a member of a drama group, etc, is desirable. Be prepared to work under pressure for long periods with tact and patience and, most essential, a sense of humour.

Appropriate qualifications are required for many specialist departments so ensure that you are doing the correct subjects for your proposed future career and remember that competition for entry to some posts or training schemes can be very keen.

Finally, the industry looks for enthusiasm—without it, forget television as a career.

Amusing incidents

During a camera rehearsal for *Saturday Night at the Mill* and in the absence of the Presenter, I had to sit alongside a circus elephant

76

'driving' a jeep. She was rocking the vehicle quite alarmingly and I wasn't convinced that she'd passed her driving test.'

We were recording a cookery programme with the final dish being a rather exotic pyramid of home-made ice-cream. Obviously it had been pre-prepared and stored in a freezer. Unfortunately when it was removed for use on the set, it was quite obvious that it had frozen solid and the cookery expert would not be able to slice it without breaking the knife. The floor assistant was sent to the canteen to buy a box of wafer bars (that's all they had!) and we squashed them together with our hands to resemble the real thing. With seconds to spare, we put the 'dish' onto the set and removed the still-frozen pyramid. The presenter sliced through her 'special' ice cream with more than the usual smile on her face!

Senior Floor Manager (freelance)

Designation   SENIOR FLOOR MANAGER (FREELANCE)
Name   *Dennis Elliott*
Qualifications *None — spent most of schooldays in hospital*

Dennis worked in the theatre as a stage director and stage manager before going onto the film industry as a props man. He learnt a great deal and became third assistant director on productions for MGM before leaving and entering the television industry. He worked for many years at HTV West before joining Yorkshire Television where he's currently working as a unit manager on large scale drama productions.

Job satisfaction

1   Being in charge of a large complex unit, under the control of a director, is extremely satisfying.
2   I like working with artists and establishing a good working relationship thus enabling them to give of their best.
3   Professional pride.

Advice

Never, never give up. Try anything to get into the industry. *It isn't easy.* I went from being a stage director in theatre to being a props man in films. But I learned a great deal and finally made it as a third assistant director and I haven't stopped working since. *Keep trying.*

Designation VIDEO TAPE EDITOR, BBC TV BIRMINGHAM
Name *Michael James Bloore*
Qualifications *A level Physics and Mathematics*

Mike worked in a factory; in a garden centre and as a postman before entering the broadcasting field. He's been in the 'business' now for nine years working his way up from studio vision engineer, telecine engineer and general videotape engineer to his current position as a videotape editor. Mike enjoys his work tremendously and doesn't feel that he could be tempted into another field. In his own words 'I think television gets into your blood and I think I shall be in the industry for life!'

Job satisfaction

1 Working closely with fellow engineers and production staff.
2 Seeing a programme through from recording to transmission.
3 Making do with limited resources, and producing as polished a finished programme as possible.

Advice

Try and find out what jobs are available and what they entail and also what qualifications are required. There's no point in finding yourself in a job you don't like or in wanting a job for which you're not qualified. Also decide whether you want to work in a large centre such as the Television Centre, London, and be in a very busy but more impersonal atmosphere, or whether you would prefer a smaller centre where there's more chance of getting to know most of your colleagues.

Amusing incidents

Not amusing at the time! I was responsible for transmitting the wrong quiz programme in the Birmingham opt-out slot. This might have passed almost unnoticed except for the first time in my experience the slot was thirty-five minutes and I'd put a thirty minute programme onto the videotape machine.

I discovered my mistake when the programme was already 'on the air' so I had to ferret around and dig out a five-minute music item to fill the gap. Surprise, surprise! The ensuing mail was predominantly from folk saying how much they'd enjoyed the music!!! (I then had to edit down the thirty-five minute programme to fill the half hour slot for the following week.)

Assistant Film Editor

Designation	ASSISTANT FILM EDITOR, BBC REGIONAL TV
Name	*Christopher Waring*
Qualifications	*City of Birmingham Polytechnic Diploma*

Chris worked in graphic design for seven years before becoming a film editor with an independent firm. He then entered the BBC as an assistant editor.

Job satisfaction

All film editing is the creation of an order out of apparent chaos—often in a limited time. Chris likens editing to the carver's block of wood—you can pull anything you like from it's depths.

Advice

Take a course in any recognized film school. Then, if you can't get into the BBC straight away, work as a holiday relief assistant during vacations. In this way you'll get to know the job and the people and stand a better chance of being accepted when you next apply.

Designation DUBBING MIXER VT/FILM BBC TV
Name *David Baumber*
Qualifications *Seven O levels*
Two A levels

David has worked in television for ten years. He started as a boom operator and then progressed to grams operator and then on to dubbing.

Job satisfaction

To be in complete control of a film sound-track and to be in the position of manipulating the sound to conjure up any mood required by the director. To look at a completely different film (picture) every day and manufacture a sound track to complement the pictures without experiencing inclement weather conditions! It's like a 'window on the world, visiting different parts of the world on celluloid'!

Advice

Get a good, all round, education. You must be able to communicate with people of all classes. In my particular field, the need is for a person with an alert, aware ear; possible musical background; an interest in hi-fi or amateur recording; and a reasonably strong academic qualification in electronics. You must expect a fairly long training period before you will gain enough experience to reach a good professional position.

Amusing incidents

Seeing a boom operator climb onto a boom 30 seconds before the start of a live show who split his trousers in full view of the audience—then he had to operate the boom for half an hour in rather draughty conditions! The show must go on...

81

Principal Vision Mixer

Designation	PRINCIPAL VISION MIXER, YORKSHIRE TV
Name	*Sue James*
Qualifications	*Five O levels*
	Three A levels
	Teaching Diploma—Physical Education

Sue taught physical education for four years and also worked a couple of years for BEA, none of which was relevant to the work she now does in television. She joined Granada Television as a trainee vision mixer in 1966 and has gone on from there to become one of three principal vision mixers at Yorkshire Television. She says that she was lucky to get the original trainee's job as they're usually given to people already working for the various companies.

Job satisfaction

Working as part of a team—but with very good opportunities to develop your initiative and an individual approach to your work—only the vision mixer knows precisely when a cut will be made. *But*—the job is changing—new techniques and more and more post-production mean that the vision mixers will have to adapt.

Advice

Don't. If you're really set on the idea, then I'd suggest that you do something else first—except in the case of wanting to be a cameraman/woman where most companies put an early age limit on trainees.

Designation   SOUND TECHNICIAN, HTV WEST
Name   *Patricia Ann Belcher*
Qualifications   *Seven O levels*
RSA Stage 1 and 2 Typing

Patti joined HTV as a Post Girl, then became secretary to the assistant chief engineer. She moved on to work for the producer of the News Magazine programme in a secretarial capacity and then became a production assistant. She very much wanted to get into the Sound Department and there was great rejoicing when she eventually made it and started work as a boom operator. She's now worked in the sound department for four years, the last two of which she's been a sound technician—(a rarity for a girl to work in Sound). Ultimately she'd like to become a producer.

Job satisfaction

The variation in work—a different programme or content every day. She likes not having to work standard hours and enjoys meeting interesting people from all walks of life who come in to the studio to appear on programmes.

Advice

Don't be afraid to start at the bottom, or in a job which is not exactly what you had in mind. If you are employed in the industry doing something other than your specific aim, show as much interest as possible in the chosen section even if it means doing so in your own time. (Patti is a fine example of having put into practice what she preaches!)

Engineer

Designation	ENGINEER BBC TV PLYMOUTH
Name	*Ken Townsend*
Qualifications	*Oxford School Certificate*

Ken says that his experience in the use of circuit diagrams, wiring, fault-finding and meeting the public while working in Post Office Telephones and Engineering helped him towards the position he holds today. He started his employment with the BBC in London as a recording engineer in the Sound service, tape and disc recording and editing. Moving to Plymouth, he incorporated communications work and general duties in television. Ken's job includes work in telecine and sound, videotape recording and duties as a cameraman. Being able to work in different areas of the same field is a peculiarity of regional television. Demarcation lines are strongly defined in the large television centres. For a youngster, being able to work in these different areas is most advantageous for he (and sometimes she) would be able to decide more readily on a specialization if moving to a Network Centre.

Job satisfaction

An opportunity is provided to be part of the programme making and to meet a wide range of personalities.

Advice

You must be prepared to study hard both before and after entering the industry. Try to take an active interest in the programmes in which you become involved. Do not be afraid to voice your opinion, but be prepared to accept criticism. Learn to leave work in its place and relax when not on duty.

Designation	ENGINEER BBC TV PLYMOUTH
Name	*Roy Melhuish*
Qualifications	*City and Guilds (Electrical Engineering)*

Roy did a five year apprenticeship as an electrical engineer and then two years in the RAF as an air wireless mechanic before joining the BBC for which he's worked for fifteen years. The demarcation line on jobs in television is generally rigidly upheld but one of the more interesting aspects of being an engineer at a small station like Plymouth is that you must be experienced in several jobs, ie camera work; sound mixing; vision control; telecine; video recording; maintenance; and working in the Sound Control Room dealing with switching and maintenance.

Roy suggests that with skills in these various fields you'd be equipped to apply for many different jobs if you wished to move on to a larger station and specialize.

Job satisfaction

Roy enjoys working in the studios because it gives him the opportunity to meet people both 'in front' and behind the camera. He feels this is important because the ultimate aim of any programme is communication. To help other colleagues produce a well made and popular programme is also satisfying.

Advice

This depends on whether you are ambitious—if you are, then don't stay in one station too long. Move around the country gaining experience. If you like a well organized life with regular hours—then this isn't the job for you!

Station Assistant

Designation	REGIONAL TELEVISION STATION ASSISTANT
	BBC TV BIRMINGHAM
Name	*Nicholas A. Patten*
Qualifications	*Nine O levels*

Nick worked as an assistant stage manager (ASM) at the Bristol Old Vic before joining Radio Bristol as record librarian. Then he became a station assistant and did a great deal of 'on air' work. He aims to be a Light Entertainment producer.

Job satisfaction

The job is so varied! Like most people in the business, Nick says he loves 'the flow of adrenalin' and also working with so many different types of people both in and out of the BBC.

Advice

Nick thinks the best way into television must be through Local Radio because of the immense opportunities. He says he's 'the classic example'. He had no technical qualifications and within twelve months of joining local radio was 'on air' most days. In Nick's own words 'amazing, considering how long it would have taken to get where I am ten years ago.'

Amusing incidents

'When I began floor managing, my cues were a little too dramatic. One day whilst cueing under the lens hood of the camera I split my trousers from one side to the other—revealing all! The presenter broke into a fit of laughter—just as well it was a recording!

Designation HEAD OF PRESENTATION, WESTWARD TV
Name *David Sunderland*
Qualifications *Five O levels*

David was in the RAF for five years and says that this work was helpful to him in that it enabled him to enter broadcasting in an engineering capacity. He's worked in television for twelve years first as a telecine operator then as a transmission controller and though he's now in presentation, his ultimate goal is to work in production. He wouldn't consider leaving the industry.

Job satisfaction

Total absorption in the working day. The area of discretion covering many aspects of broadcasting with never a dull moment and no chance to get bored.

Advice

One hundred per cent determination to be part of the broadcasting industry together with any qualifications and abilities that one can show to one's advantage, but it has been my experience that those who really want to get in, eventually do!

Amusing incidents

Westward do their *Epilogues* 'live' and the studio is often shared by the outgoing announcer, who may be doing the weather forecast, and the incoming cleric. One of these religious gentlemen was winding up some clockwork toys to be used as visual aids in his talk. Obviously assuming that if you're not seen, you're not heard, he let go of a toy. Imagine the announcer's consternation as a 'frog' bobbed across the desk in front of him!

Designation   PROMOTIONS AND CONTINUITY SCRIPTWRITER
WESTWARD TV
Name   *Stuart Hutchison*
Qualifications   *School Certificate (six credits, two passes)*
Higher School Certificate (English and Biology)

Stuart was an actor before entering television. (He also plays drums.) He has worked as an announcer/presenter/newsreader and interviewer. He might have gone on working in this capacity but the promotions scriptwriter went on holiday—Stuart stepped into the breach and decided he actually enjoyed writing, even if he couldn't spell! He's perfectly happy with his work, would leave the industry with extreme reluctance, and really only wants to do what he's doing but to have more facilities.

Job satisfaction

He thinks of each promotion spot as a small production and thoroughly enjoys collecting together the material and writing the script for a particular performer. He attempts to make the promotion spots as entertaining as possible.

Advice

Don't give up. It's very frustrating trying to start in broadcasting. Take any job connected with it. You can't know too much about any aspects of broadcasting. You can usually transfer to what you ultimately want—or you may well find that you like what you're doing instead.

Film Director (freelance)

Designation   FILM DIRECTOR (FREELANCE)
Name   *Ian McFarlane*
Qualifications *None*

Ian started work at 16 as assistant cameraman for Ace Films in Wardour Street—his pay was £3.5s 6d for a seven day week! His job entailed making tea, polishing the cameraman's shoes, cleaning cameras, putting out dustbins and generally being pushed around! Then followed a four year period being trained as an assistant cameraman (proper)! and learning how films are made. Then at 21 Ian became a Cameraman for the NCB making training films in coal mines, and at 23 he directed his first film—a twenty-minute documentary. Then he went into television as a cameraman shooting over fifty *World in Action* films in 'trouble spots' around the world, also one hour documentaries for both Independent Companies and the BBC.

In 1968 Ian began directing and filming over sixty programmes in twelve war zones and many trouble areas of the world for *This Week*. He also directed two drama series for Yorkshire Television and has worked on numerous *Whicker's World* programmes. 1975 saw Ian setting up a small film company which made a two hour film on the Third World called *Five Minutes to Midnight* and also a trilogy on Iran *In Search of Democracy*. (This latter programme, at the time of writing, hasn't been shown in England.) Most recently there's been a series of six *Whicker's World* programmes in India.

Job satisfaction

Lies in the opportunities to entertain and inform others.

Advice

Be a good listener, but above all develop powers of observation and sensitivity to people and places.

Art Director (freelance)

Designation   ART DIRECTOR (FREELANCE)
Name   *Michael Minas*
Qualifications   *National Dipoloma in Design*

Michael has spent all fourteen years of his working life in television where he started as a scenic artist. After a period with Thames Television, Michael is now'operating as a freelance. He says his goal is to undertake art-directing and directing a film. When asked how far off these achievements are, he replied 'They're coming'.

Job satisfaction

Michael says he believes very much in his own ideas and when these are *bought*, (very important), used, and broadcast unchanged, then he's fully satisfied. If there's no room for using his imagination on a job then he's dissatisfied. He also says that he likes working with people who are one hundred per cent devoted to what they're doing.

Advice

Never underestimate your capabilities. If there's something you can't do, there are always others who can help you out or do it for you. I recommend the latter—it allows you more time to get on with the next project. If you have any sign of imagination—develop it.

Amusing incidents

My first design for television—I filled the studio with an enormous set—and completely forgot to allow room for the cameras!! It was good to look at but *unshootable*!

I obtained permission from the owners of a house in SW London to remove all the leaves from their trees to provide a winter background for a play which we were shooting in the middle of July. Three hours later, when nearly half the job was completed, I discovered, to my horror, that the men had gone to the wrong house. I had arranged (on the telephone) for them to go to number seventeen, but unfortunately they harvested the garden of number seventy. The owners of the house weren't very amused but well compensated—a lesson from experience!

Designation	NEWSREADER: BBC TV
	RADIO 4 PRESENTER
	START THE WEEK AND BAKER'S DOZEN
Name	*Richard Baker*
Qualifications	*MA Cantab (History and Modern Languages)*

Richard did a year of teaching and another year of acting before joining the BBC as a studio manager. He quickly became a Radio 3 (then the Third Programme) announcer and has worked steadily through the years to the position he holds today as one of our most respected newsreaders and programme presenters.

In 1972, 1974 and yet again in 1979 he received the TV Newscaster of the Year award, presented by the Radio Industries Club of Great Britain.

Job satisfaction

Richard says that in newsreading the reward comes from making a clear presentation of facts, and coping with frequent technical problems. In chairing a programme like *Start the Week*, it's a question of maintaining a balance and keeping things going. In any broadcasting, the satisfaction comes from feeling you have *communicated clearly*.

Advice

'Some experience elsewhere is very useful if you are not to be too confined within the World of the Media which is all too apt to be self-contained and self satisfied.'

Amusing incident

The boy who asked for an autograph outside Broadcasting House:

RB: Do you know who I am?
Boy: No, who are you?
RB: I'm a newsreader.
Boy: Never mind!

Presenter

Designation   PRESENTER *TOMORROW'S WORLD:* BBC TV
                       RISK BUSINESS
Name   *Judith Hann*
Qualifications   *BSc Zoology*

Judith got basic training as a science writer in newspapers. She worked as a science writer for ten years before entering the field of broadcasting where she contributed to a science spot on Radio 4 and reported on scientific issues for a children's news programme before joining *Tomorrow's World* as a presenter/interviewer.

Job satisfaction

Finding a story, following it through and presenting it in an interesting way is most satisfying for Judith. Her ultimate goal is to produce programmes and she says she wouldn't consider leaving the industry yet.

Advice
Get good background training—beginning with as much education as possible. Then make a start in newspapers or broadcasting and learn everything from the basics.

Designation	PRESENTER OF *PEBBLE MILL* AND *SATURDAY NIGHT AT THE MILL*, BBC TV
Name	*Bob Langley*
Qualifications	*None*

Bob worked in many different fields during the early part of his working life. He did many labouring jobs and even worked as a lumberjack in Canada. None of these jobs was even remotely relevant to television although it must have given Bob a wide view of life. He's now worked in the medium for twelve years, starting as a scriptwriter with Tyne Tees in Newcastle. After a year he went in front of the camera as anchor man on the Regional News Magazine Programme. From Tyne Tees he moved to London and joined the BBC as a National Newsreader. Next came a job as roving reporter for the *24 Hours* programme. A period on *Nationwide* followed and then Bob moved on to *Pebble Mill*—a lunchtime magazine programme—where he's worked as an interviewer/presenter for several years.

Bob says that the most surprising job offer was his initial one in television as a scriptwriter because this is the kind of post normally offered to someone already making a living in the literary world. (I think Bob is being ultra modest as he now has several published books to his credit—so the talent was always there!) He says that the scriptwriting job not only presented him with a springboard for other more ambitious projects but it also gave him a thorough grounding in all aspects of broadcasting.

Job satisfaction

Working in television is a bit like riding a roller-coaster at a very fast speed. When you look at the dips ahead, you wish you could find some way of jumping off, but after a while you realize you've become an addict. (A sentiment I share entirely!) The satisfaction of the job is too momentary and ephemeral to sustain anyone for very long, but in a curious corkscrew way, that's one of its good points. There isn't time to sit around feeling proud of yourself. You're only as good as your last programme, and the next is around the corner. *Excitement* is the keyword—the knowledge that you're working to a deadline and when the moment comes you must go on the air in front of umpteen million people. Always, there's that elusive thrill of working in the most powerful communications medium known to man. Bob adds—'Of course, you have to learn to live with ulcers and hardening arteries!'

Advice

There's only one safe way to enter television. First, find a job that is in some way relevant to what you eventually want to do. For example, if your ultimate goal is to be a Current Affairs producer, or a television reporter, try and get a start on your local newspaper. If it's the Make-up Department that attracts you, see if there's a vacancy at your nearest beautician. When the time comes to make a direct approach to a television company, don't be over-ambitious. Try the Regional Stations first. They're more likely to have vancancies and more likely to give you a try. Too many people go immediately for the 'big-time'. Learn to walk before you run. You can always move to the Network later.

Designation   BROADCASTER (FREELANCE)
Name   *Anne Nightingale*
Qualifications   *Eight O levels*
                   Diploma of journalism from polytechnic course

Annie started work on a weekly paper in Brighton. She also wrote a music column and did interviews for radio programmes like *Today* and *Woman's Hour*. She got bitten by the radio 'bug' and wanted to combine this with her interest in music. To become a disc jockey was almost impossible. She knocked on the doors of the BBC continually until eventually she gave up hope and returned to Brighton to work on a magazine programme for local radio. Then she heard that the Beeb was looking for a woman disc jockey—so she sent in a tape of her programme and was offered a trial run. She did a few programmes and then the economy axe fell—temporarily. She filled in her time with writing and local radio until she was offered a Sunday afternoon slot on Radio 1 (which had previously been the Dave Lee Travis Request Show) which she occupied for four years. Over a decade Annie has built up an excellent reputation and she's worked on a wide variety of radio programmes. At the time of writing she's also the presenter of BBC TV's *Old Grey Whistle Test*.

Job satisfaction

Plenty! In radio you get a very pure form of communication. 'What I say into the microphone comes out at the other end entirely uncut, un-edited, moved around or censored. You can create a far more precise meaning using voice inflection than could ever be (for me) effective through the printed word. I'm doing what I enjoy doing and I wouldn't want it to stop.'

Advice

Apparently, not many girls want to be disc jockeys, but my advice to both girls and boys is to study hard at school. (More and more DJs are doing interviews on their shows and you can't do that if you haven't a fairly wide general knowledge.) Perhaps get a job in a record shop; accumulate knowledge of various aspects of music; run a disco; try to get a job with local radio, however menial, and work your way up from there.

95

Broadcaster (freelance)

Amusing incidents

When Terry Wogan was on Radio One, he would hand over to me. He had a 'Spot the Deliberate Mistake Competition' and I ruined it by not realising this, and pointing out his 'error' on air!

Acknowledgment to plates between pages 96 and 97

Production team filming on location
BBC copyright

Cameraman, outside broadcasts
HTV West copyright

The joys of filming in the rain!
A documentary with Johnny Morris
HTV West copyright

Floor manager
Thames Television copyright

Make-up artists
Thames Television copyright

Videotape editor
Thames Television copyright

Sound and cameramen
Thames Television copyright

New dubbing console
HTV West copyright

Filming Georgie Fame with his group
HTV West copyright

Interior of studio
Thames Television copyright

Interviewer, Marian Foster, at Pebble Mill
BBC copyright

Newsreader, Richard Baker
By kind permission of the BBC

South studio
Thames Television copyright

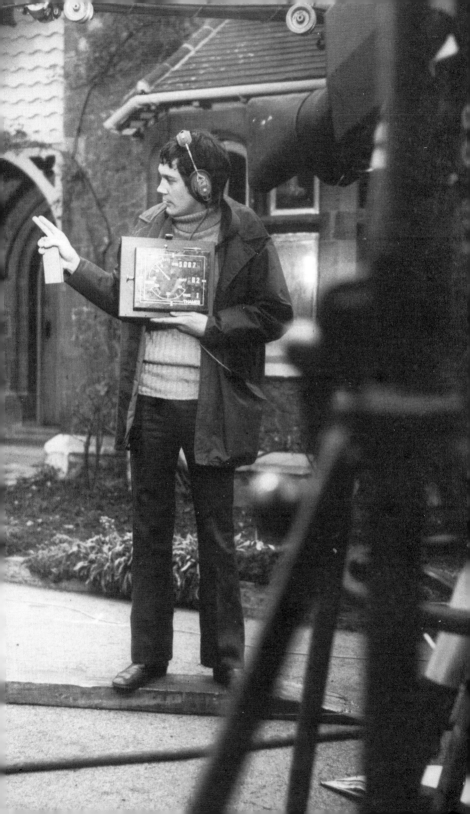

Designation   BROADCASTER (FREELANCE)
Name   *Noel Edmunds*
Qualifications *Ten O levels*
                  Three A levels
                  and swam the length of the baths!

Noel did one year of student teaching at an East End primary school and say this could be regarded as a help with regard to his attitude towards *Swap Shop* (BBC TV). He was with Radio Luxembourg for a year and has spent ten with BBC Radio One. He's also done a great deal of television working on programmes such as *Come Dancing*! (his exclamation mark not mine) *Top of the Pops*; *Top Gear*; *Call My Bluff*; *Nationwide*; *Juke Box Jury*; *The Boat Show*; and latterly *The Multi-Coloured Swap Shop*. He says that his ambition is 'To be a very, very old broadcaster'.

Job satisfaction

'If one is allowed to momentarily ignore the element of egotism in my work, the most satisfactory aspect of my present situation is the 'team' atmosphere. Admittedly a small team in the radio sense but particularly with television I enjoy a privileged position presenting the labours and talents of many 'back room' people'.

Advice

Be prepared to wait for the right moment. Push too hard too soon and you'll probably miss the really big opportunity. When you get that lesson learnt, just remember a moving target is more difficult to hit. A little humility can be a big asset!

Broadcaster (freelance)

Designation   BROADCASTER (FREELANCE)
Name   *Andy Peebles*
Qualifications   *Five O levels*
    National Diploma—Hotel Management

Andy took an hotel management course directly he left school. He spent a year working in hotels which is hardly relevant to the work he now does as a disc jockey/interviewer, except that he was dealing with people. Realising that the Hotel World was not for him, Andy left and spent six years working in discotheques in London, Bournemouth and Manchester. He then joined BBC Local Radio in Manchester where he worked for a year before signing up with the opposition—Radio Piccadilly. He remained in Manchester for over four years doing news and sport presentation, interview work and music programmes before joining BBC Radio 1 as a DJ in 1979.

Job satisfaction

Anyone without an ego of sorts should instantly dismiss broadcasting as a career.

Meeting people is one of the biggest stimulants to me. At national level, the financial rewards are substantial although one should always remember that the catalyst is one's time on air.

Advice

If you honestly believe you have something to offer in radio then get into it as early as you can. Hospital radio is a great springboard. You may need to take a back seat for a while but the experience will be invaluable. Above all, belief in yourself is the ultimate credential.

Training schemes

Having read this far and you still want to work in Television, where do you start? Well, first of all, I suggest that you give serious thought early on in your secondary education, to the area of television in which you wish to work because, for certain jobs, there are specific qualifications and the sooner you stream academically in the right direction the better. Also you could try writing to your local television or radio station to ask whether they would be prepared to let you make a visit. I should add that not too many companies are prepared to do this, mainly because of the pressures of their production output—but it's worth a try! From time to time there are television shows which have invited audiences and it's well worth trying to get tickets in order to 'see how it's done'.

As the BBC and the Independent Television Companies have different ways of operating and also required slightly differing qualifications for jobs, I'll deal with them separately starting with the BBC and the areas in which they offer training.

BBC TRAINING SCHEMES

Engineering

In the engineering area, staffing falls into two basic groups
1   *Technical operators* who deal with cameras, sound, lighting, etc, and
2   *Engineers 'proper'* who make sure technical equipment works, does the job for which it's designed and repair and modify the technical 'hardware'. This group also mans some of the control rooms and operates some of the more sophisticated equipment such as videotape recorders. For both intakes, the BBC prefers to recruit straight from school and train staff itself. This means that a boy, or girl for that matter, should be reasonably competent in maths and science.

Training Schemes

With regard to *technical operators*, technical aptitude is only part of the entry requirement. There must be a strong interest in audio visuals, eg a related hobby such as photography or tape recording. The entrants will be aged 17/18 and will undergo lengthy periods of residential training at the BBC School at Evesham interspersed with on-the-job training.

A *'Sound' trainee* would then graduate to rigging microphone cables etc then to Sound assistant operating a microphone boom in a studio. The next step would be working as a tape gram operator—selecting and playing-in sound effects, and then on to being a sound supervisor who mixes and balances sound in the studio and is in charge of overall sound coverage on productions.

A *'Vision' trainee* would begin by pushing around the cameras and looking after the camera cables, gradually progressing to junior cameraman. There's a parallel career shoot which comes off the camera side of operations and that's visual operation—which means work in the control gallery assisting in the lighting of productions. The senior job on this side is a Technical Manager who, as well as being the lighting specialist, is also in charge of the technical operations team for that production.

The *Engineer 'proper'* must have more clearly defined qualifications. These can be gained internally (preferred) or externally. In the former case, an applicant of 17/18, with a good background in maths and physics, would be trained by the BBC with orientation, of course, towards BBC requirements. The external requirement is for City and Guilds, Higher National Certificate or a degree in electronics and the applicant would be in the early twenties age group. The engineering course is more academic than that for a technical operator and at the end of the training there's an examination which *must be passed* before the BBC will employ the trainee as an engineer. These trainees are called Technical Assistants.

The BBC also requires technicians on the mechanical side trained in instrument making. For any youngsters interested, the field is wide open. The Corporation offers limited training and prefers the applicant to have been trained externally in mechanical skills, say at one of the Government Skill Centres or in private industry.

Make-up

The applicant should have a good educational background, preferably with A level in English and art and A or O level history.

100

Emphasis is also placed on a pleasant personality and the ability to deal tactfully and sympathetically with all types of people. And there must be a proven interest in make-up for television, theatre or film and/or training in hairdressing, beauty culture or art. It also helps to have done work with amateur dramatic or operatic societies from both the practical aspect and the necessity of dealing with temperamental folk under pressure. Candidates invited for an interview should be prepared to take a practical test. Those selected for the two years' training spend a three month trial period at the BBC School in London and are tested at the end of the first and third months before taking up the practical duties of the job.

Research assistant trainees

(This is the only training scheme giving direct entry to television production.)

These traineeships are intended to provide BBC Television with a reserve of trained research assistants, principally for factual and educational programmes. Applicants should be between the ages of 20 and 30 with a degree *or* considerable general experience of television production, *or* firm evidence of journalistic ability. They must also be able to display a broad range of interests including at least some of the following: writing, including journalism; political, economic, social and international affairs, science and technology; music and the Arts; history and archaeology; entertainment; education, including teaching; travel and languages, film-making; organising ability. Competition for these traineeships is exceptionally high—less than two per cent of applicants are offered a place. Training takes place over eighteen months and the trainee is free to compete for Research Assistant posts during this period.

News trainees

Trainees are recruited largely from the universities but the scheme is open to non-graduates with good academic qualifications and evidence of relevant journalistic experience. The training lasts for up to two years and the comprehensive course is intended to qualify the candidate as a professional journalist to work in radio and television newsrooms, both national and regional; the External Services Newsroom; Local Radio; and programmes such as *Nationwide*, *Today*, *World at One* and *Today in Parliament*.

The first six months of the course are spent in Broadcasting House in London. This part includes instruction in basic newswriting and tape recording; news production; the techniques of reporting, interviewing and broadcasting, and the law as it affects journalists—also an intensive course in Teeline shorthand.

After the initial six months, the course continues at Television Centre in West London. Here the trainees learn the basic techniques of television news, such as writing to film, the use of stills and graphics, handling video-tape, and editing and camera work.

The second year of training consists of a series of working attachments each of three months, to various parts of the BBC in London and the regions.

Approximately ten trainees are taken on in a year—so competition is keen.

Film training

These schemes are designed to equip trainees to work as assistant film cameramen; assistant film recordists; assistant film editors; and film assistants class II (projectionists). (Of course prospects exist for promotion to full film cameraman, editor, recordist and film assistant class 1 by means of competition internally when vacancies occur.)

Candidates should have a good general education equal to O level standard, and it is essential for them to show a genuine and lively interest in films and the technique of film making and to be able to support this with practical evidence such as membership of a film-making society, and in the case of recording an interest in tape recording and tape electronics. Lower age limit for applicants is 18 and the preferred upper limit is usually 25.

Personnel trainees

Occasionally the BBC recruits young graduates to train as personnel officers, preferably those with a year or so of full-time relevant work experience. Candidates spend up to two years attached to a variety of departments in a working capacity. They attend internal training courses and are also expected to study for the IPM diploma, for which they are given day release. Towards the end of their second year, trainees will be expected to apply under the BBC's open competitive appointments system.

What the BBC is looking for as trainee material is a person with a good degree; a positive interest in public service broadcasting; a demonstrable commitment to work in Personnel; the ability to deal not only with people but with essential routine tasks of salary administration, recruitment and cessations; paperwork associated with employment legislation, etc, and a balanced and mature personality with the capacity for objective judgement and wide general interests.

———————

These areas are those in which the BBC offers a training scheme. They are only too willing to send out brochures and leaflets covering other fields of employment. For example, at the time of waiting, I have over twenty 'handouts' covering everything from engineering, through design and costume design to opportunities for librarians and secretarial staff. (List of brochures available and addresses for application on page 106).

The appointments officer to whom I spoke with regard to employment in the BBC was anxious that I should communicate some basic advice to my young readers. One must have specified qualifications for any job, and television is no exception. Although the necessary qualifications are preferred for a job in, let's say, film, costume department, make-up, and scenic design, other attributes such as creativity, initiative, enthusiasm and very important 'commitment'—these may tip the balance in your favour.

Another point which was stressed was that if you should fail to be offered a place on a BBC Training Scheme (and competition is *very tough*) then don't give up. The competition is not between you and the BBC it's between you and the other person who just had the edge on you. So go off and get some experience. For example, work as a journalist on a paper, if it's a news or research traineeship you've set your sights on; do a beauty or hairdressing course to help you towards a job in make-up; join a film-making society if it's the film side of television which attracts you.

Don't forget that once you are 'inside' working for the BBC, it is easier to apply for other positions which are regularly exhibited on the 'Staff Vacancy' board. Remember the advice of several contributors to this book—if you can't get the job you want, take another one at a lower level and work like mad to achieve your primary goal.

INDEPENDENT TELEVISION TRAINING SCHEMES

There are fifteen independent television programme companies operating throughout Britain and Northern Ireland. They have a contract with the Independent Broadcasting Authority (IBA) to provide the programmes which the IBA then transmit over regions of the country. Most of these companies train individuals for their particular requirements as and when the need arises, but few except Thames Television operate a training *scheme* as such. Much of the independent companies' training is for employees already working in the company in order to increase their efficiency and to aid them in their career progression.

Thames Television hand out excellent information with regard to their training schemes and also list the basic qualifications they would require in order to consider an applicant for a job. On reading through their leaflets, I gained the impression that on the whole they prefer to take in staff a year or two older than the age range preferred by the BBC.

Let's take a look at the main training schemes run by Thames.

Technical training scheme

This course covers those who are interested in camera work, sound and technical operations and television engineering. All trainees do the same basic course with an emphasis on their own specialist subject.

Candidates are usually between the ages of twenty and twenty five and must have some relevant experience in close circuit studios, recording studios, equipment manufacture or other allied industries. Alternatively the candidate must have successfully completed a course at a specialist college dealing with Film, Television or Communication Engineering. An interest in activities such as amateur dramatics, and cine and photographic clubs or projects is also looked for in prospective candidates for the training course.

The course lasts for a year and consists of a broad-based training in most aspects of the technical, operational and creative subjects. The course is divided into two six-month periods. The first is spent at the Company's Training Centre at Teddington and the second period is spent on attachments to all the operational areas. At the end of the course trainees go on to junior positions working at the studio centre at Teddington, the Mobile Division at Hanworth or the transmission centre at Euston.

Make-up

Candidates need to be at least 21 and have a good educational background including O levels in, for example, Art, Literature and History. They should also have completed a course in beauty therapy, make-up and hairdressing. (The London College of Fashion is one establishment which provides a suitable course.) Because the make-up artist must work in all weather conditions, physical fitness is a necessary requirement and the unsociability of working hours is stressed.

Production assistants

The production assistant needs to have shorthand and typing to secretarial standards and a good sense of mental arithmetic, and a keen eye for detail and accuracy. The assistant must be over 21, be prepared to travel and work very unsociable hours! Trainee production assistants are selected from existing staff with the necessary qualifications who are able to deal with stressful situations. The obvious way into this kind of job is through secretarial work at a high and competent level.

Secretarial trainees

Trainees are usually college leavers between the ages of 18 and 20, with minimum speeds of 100 wpm shorthand and 50 wpm typewriting and with an O level standard of education. The period of training is a minimum of nine months and a maximum of twelve months. After a period in the Training Centre the secretaries are moved around the Company deputising for experienced secretaries in various departments and eventually they will be offered a permanent secretarial position.

These are the areas in which Thames Television offers training schemes but they also have a comprehensive list of information covering other areas of television work such as design, graphic design, stage management, floor management, etc, which lists their basic requirements before a candidate would be considered for a position with the Company.

In 1979 the IBA started a Trainee Scheme for Broadcast Transmitter Engineers. Candidates must have a Higher National Certificate or Higher Technical Certificate, or an equivalent qualification in Electrical or Electronic Engineering. Fifteen to twenty candidates are accepted for the eighteen month course. Practical training is carried out at the IBA Establishment at Seaton in Devon, and Academic training is undertaken at Newcastle

Polytechnic. Details of the course can be obtained from the IBA at Crawley, Hampshire.

I haven't dealt with every job one can do in television—it would require an encyclopaedia! But I have tried to pick out the most obvious 'streams' in which I think most of you will show an initial interest.

I don't want to burden you or your pocket with an enormous booklist but I strongly recommend that you get hold of the following which are invaluable for giving an insight into the workings of the world of television:

BBC Handbook, British Broadcasting Corporation

Television and Radio 19—Independent Broadcasting Authority

(Both these books are brought out annually with the new edition appearing at the end of the previous year)

Education and Training for Film and Television—BKSTS.

Television Studio, Judy Lever, McDonald Insider Series.

Where to write

For information regarding qualifications and training schemes on the Engineering side of the BBC:
The Engineering Recruitment Officer
BBC, Broadcasting House
London, W1A 1AA

For all other appointments and training scheme information:
Appointments Department
BBC, Broadcasting House
London W1A 1AA

For information with regard to qualifications, and training schemes run by Thames Television:
Thames Television Limited
Teddington Studios
Teddington Lock
Teddington TW11 9NT
Middlesex

For addresses of Local Radio, and Regional Television Stations, both BBC and Independent, use your local phone directory.

And for information on the IBA Trainee Scheme:
Course Administrator
Trainee Broadcast Transmission Engineers
Independent Broadcasting Authority
Crawley Court, Crawley
Near Winchester, Hampshire

Index